Enter the wintry landscapes of the Arctic, mysterious caves in the Red Rocks and the whirling vortexes of Sedona to be transported through the mystical portals of your soul through Rosanna's writing. Bear witness to the profound soul connection and hidden wisdom deep within each of us. Rosanna reveals the many ways in which to become sovereign over oneself while seeking healing and enlightenment. A must-read for all in the modern world.

My experience with Rosanna's healing shamanic journey weekend was nothing less than profound. Through the medicine of journey work over the course of those powerful few days with her, I cracked myself wide open, making space for a whole new person to emerge. This was the beginning of evolving personally, professionally and more spiritually than ever before. I am deeply grateful to Rosanna.
**Tosca Reno,** *New York Times* and international best-selling author and Founder of *Eat-Clean Revolution*

The moment I began reading this book, I couldn't put it down. There are many unexpected twists and turns weaved into the events that unfold. Rosanna's visions come alive with a rich language that she uses to paint enchanting images of what it's like to commune with ancient spirits.

Her experiences are beautifully expressed and are relevant to those of us who are trying to understand our place in the universe and the meaning of life.

Rosanna's closeness to her spirit guides and the loving encouragement and enlightenment they give her leave me feeling reassured and supported. She has once again given the world remarkable insight into what trusting our guides can really mean, and how it can help us to make the most of our opportunities and decisions.

This is the most inspiring book I have read in a very long time, I am recommending it to all of my family and friends.

**Victoria Sheridan,** rejuvenation coach, speaker, and author of *Rejuvenate Your Life*

Rosanna Ienco brought us into a magical odyssey with her first book and takes us even deeper with *Enter the Journey: A Mystical Guide for Rebirth and Renewal*.

Rosanna uses creative visualizations to open readers to their wild imagination which is so needed to transport us into the mysteries that are waiting for us, as we learn we are truly interdimensional beings and that there are landscapes here on Earth that have portals that lead to mystical odysseys with loving spirit teachers.

Rosanna takes us into the vortexes of Sedona and into the Australian Outback known for hidden knowledge.

*Enter the Journey* is a remarkable book about rebirth and renewal and creating a strong relationship with nature and spirits that are here to help us on our remarkable journey through life.

**Sandra Ingerman MA,** shamanic teacher and award-winning author of twelve books including *Walking in Light* and *The Book of Ceremony*

When working with new authors and existing, experienced authors, I often advise them to create a valuable, useful, unique book that will positively uplift the reader. Rosanna has done just that with this wonderful masterpiece. The subtitle is completely appropriate as this book is designed to renew and uplift your life. Enjoy the journey of the author's experiences as she will inspire you to look at life in a truly unique way that can invite peace into your heart.

**Peggy McColl,** *New York Times* best-selling author of *Your Destiny Switch*

Some writers will tell you about the journey to self-transcendence, but Rosanna takes you on the journey with her. With each sojourn she describes, you will find yourself reaching deeper and deeper into the sacred inner realm within you. If you are drawn to shamanic journeys and sacred odysseys of the soul, then this book is a must-read.

**Denise Linn,** best-selling author of *Soul Coaching* and *Sacred Space*, internationally renowned teacher, founder of Linn Academy and world acclaimed expert in Feng Shui

In *Enter the Journey*, brilliant writer Rosanna Ienco brings to life vivid images of visions, shamanic journeys, and spectacular locations as if we were indeed travelling with her in the physical and spiritual world. In this mystical guide, we are taken into the underworld through magical caves and into intricate vortexes and portals where she reveals to the readers how significant it is to meet our own spirit guides. Through poetic storytelling and creative visualization, we are enlightened, uplifted and awakened to a new journey and existing reality.

I believe that Rosanna's cultural background from the region of Calabria in Southern Italy is part of her magical quality, being that Calabria is indeed the land of seers and healers. This book is a must-read for anyone interested in the true power of shamanic journeys and healing through vision quests, showing us how our spirit allies will always be there for us and accompany us if we allow them.

**Alessandra Belloni,** best-selling author of *Healing Journeys with the Black Madonna*, singer, percussionist and teacher of Southern Italian folk traditions

# Enter the Journey

A Mystical Guide for Rebirth
and Renewal

# Enter the Journey

## A Mystical Guide for Rebirth and Renewal

Rosanna Ienco

BOOKS

Winchester, UK
Washington, USA

JOHN HUNT PUBLISHING

First published by O-Books, 2023
O-Books is an imprint of John Hunt Publishing Ltd., 3 East St., Alresford,
Hampshire SO24 9EE, UK
office@jhpbooks.com
www.johnhuntpublishing.com
www.o-books.com

For distributor details and how to order please visit the 'Ordering' section on our website.

Text copyright: Rosanna Ienco 2022

ISBN: 978 1 80341 098 2
978 1 80341 099 9 (ebook)
Library of Congress Control Number: 2022936523

A CIP catalogue record for this book is available from the British Library.

Design: Stuart Davies

UK: Printed and bound by CPI Group (UK) Ltd, Croydon, CR0 4YY
Printed in North America by CPI GPS partners

We operate a distinctive and ethical publishing philosophy in
all areas of our business, from our global network of authors to
production and worldwide distribution.

# Contents

**Previous Title**
*Awakening the Divine Soul: Finding Your Life Purpose*
ISBN: 978-1846941542

For my precious children,
Keanu, Aragorn and Amethyst, the absolute loves of my life
and my greatest teachers.
You are my sun, my moon and my stars. I love you to
eternity...

# Author's Note

This book and the exercises and meditations within are in no way a substitute for therapy or medical advice. If you have any medical conditions, seek the advice of a professional healthcare provider. Some locations mentioned in this book may not be suitable for everyone. Please seek medical advice from a practitioner and, when necessary, a tour guide to make sure you are safe to visit.

Check for adverse weather conditions before planning any trip. The author is in no way responsible or liable for your actions, the way you use the information contained herein, or the effects that may arise from performing the given exercises, meditations and ceremony rituals and celebrations.

Some of my personal experiences while in a meditative or altered state of awareness are not based on any real events or teachings from any Indigenous cultures but are described purely as they were shown during my own meditations and drum journeys.

# Preface

*Enter the Journey* is an invitation to expand your imagination far beyond your perception. It is a guidebook filled with poetic and adventurous stories. When you enter that sacred place within your creative visualization, you enter a portal of possibilities. A place where your interior and exterior landscapes merge into a beautiful creation.

The earth is an abundant place with limitless experiences for you to make your own. We are beyond blessed to be graced with the most magnificent scenery, one of nature's true gifts. There are some places in the world that are healing portals that can support your spiritual journey. Sedona, Arizona is one of those places, where people from all around the world make their pilgrimage. I have met so many kindred spirits and have shared miraculous stories of transformation. I have personally witnessed miracles and healing through the many vortexes and caves I have visited.

I would like to acknowledge the Native American, First Peoples and Indigenous people from all over the world for sharing their incredible lands with myself and others who are so very blessed to walk on their sacred territory. I have been called back to Sedona numerous times during a period of over twenty years. Each time I visit, the more the land speaks to me. This book came together to share my uplifting experiences and to invite you to have your own encounters whether you decide to visit in person or simply connect through the essence of this book.

I invite you to enter the journey as I take you through many portals and caves. You will discover that you do not walk this earth alone. There is an abundance of guardians in the form of spirit animals and guides. The elements of the earth will also truly support you on your journey. Nature will always speak to you if you allow it. If you listen to the whispers in the wind, you will be guided to places you have not yet been.

As you move through these chapters, take your time and pace yourself to best suit where you may currently be in your life. Remember to pause as required to partake in the guided meditations and exercises offered within each chapter. Always listen to your own guidance and the wisdom of your body, mind, spirit and soul.

*May you have many beautiful blessings along the way.*

Love, Rosanna

# Introduction ~ Drum Ceremony Intention

The soul of the earth is pulsing; can you feel it? She calls to your very essence. As I beat the drum, every vibration aligns with my own heartbeat. I play in honor of our great mother, also honoring you and your pulse, celebrating your life's journey.

Are you ready to embrace your divinity? Some part of you was drawn to pick up this book. Maybe this is the divine timing for your new journey of rebirth and renewal. Be still for a moment and breathe deeply. I invite you on your very own sacred pilgrimage of transformation. Together we will enter mysterious caves and deeply connect with the spirit allies that guided me on this adventure. Are you ready for a magical journey? We will embrace the spirit, the very soul of the enchanting lands deep within the mysterious red rocks of Sedona, Arizona. The spirits of the land want to be heard and remembered, as well as being honored and respected. This book you are holding is a mystical guide that will take you on many new and exciting adventures. As you delve deeper, be patient with yourself and remember to take your time with the meditations and rituals I will guide you through. I encourage you to take a pause when you feel you need to and then come back to the book when you are guided to do so.

As you move through each chapter, may you realign to your own natural rhythm of life. May you also loosen your grip and have the courage to let go of whatever may be blocking you from living an authentic life, one that is aligned with your heart's desires.

As we enter powerful portals, may you find personal empowerment and liberation as each cave and vortex generously offers inspiration and wisdom for you to carry forward on your path of courage and transformation. Together we will enter new portals of possibilities. Stay open to receiving the blessings that are all around you. You will have many opportunities to move through stagnant energy, to break through any areas of your life where you feel stuck. This is where we recreate new beginnings. Your life was meant to be filled with joy and wonder. Do you remember when you stopped dreaming?

As you journey through this book, you will create your own reality by designing a new life. As I continue to drum, may you feel the presence of mother earth through your own heartbeat. At times, your path may become arduous, but please don't give up, and strive to keep moving forward. I know this because I have been there myself, and still stumble at times. Just know that this is where you will find your greatest strength, and who you truly are.

The book will take you through four parts. Part one is introspection as you journey through the heart and walk between the worlds. Part two is all about integration as you begin to see the true reflection of who you really are. Part three is interweaving as you enter the shaman's cave and the wisdom lodge to take part in a ritual of rebirth. Part four will take you into the deeper depths of your imagination from a mystical rainforest to an emerald lake where you will renew your spirit in a ceremony of celebration.

Have the courage to stay on track. Break through all the barriers that have been preventing you from achieving a life of full potential. If you can imagine it, you can create it. This book will help you explore the power of your imagination and the inner realms of your soul. You will be amazed how your life will unfold. May you have bountiful blessings on your transformational path to rebirth and renewal.

Rosanna Ienco
Sedona, Arizona

Through the Vastness of Nothingness comes Eternity...

# Part I

# Introspection

# Chapter One

# The Journey Continues

*The veil is always present; it is in the moment you choose to lift it that you will be given new insight.*

There was stillness in the air, it was cool and crisp. Tranquility overtook this wintery scene. The aurora borealis was dancing in the sky, swirling green and white streamers reflecting off the surface of a frozen lake, a clear and perfect mirror where a polar bear was waiting to greet me.

The mystical colors of the northern lights began whirling through me as I walked towards this huge bear. The crunching sound of snow underneath my feet calmed me, it felt familiar and reminded me of the walks I took to elementary school. It was as if I was a young child again – quiet, anxious and sensitive.

Each step brought me closer to what would be an exhilarating adventure. The veil was becoming thin between the earthly plane and this one, the spirit world. I was entering an altered state through my deep breathing and relaxation. It was a place of deep serenity and I felt safe.

My intuition told me that the polar bear was a pregnant female, she looked almost ready to hibernate before giving birth to her cubs in the new year. Perhaps she wanted a final moment of play before entering her den, a protected and warm place where she would hide away with her newborn cubs until springtime.

The last time I saw her, she was taking me for a swim underneath the ocean. I will never forget our last encounter as it forever changed my life. Her name is Tundra, she taught me how to trust the invisible world and that which can sometimes never be defined or explained – the spirit world, that other realm that has become a natural part of my life.

As a walker between the worlds, it can sometimes become challenging and easy to doubt. We are always seeking proof to validate our experiences. It's like a muscle that gets stronger over the years; as you travel through these journeys, and delve into deeper meditations, you will become clearer in your vision, your intuition will become your compass. It will be harder to question when everything starts to fall into place. Trusting is key, no one knows more than your own wisdom. Learning to trust it is your task.

Tundra told me to climb onto her back. Her fur felt a little rough against my delicate hands. I wrapped my arms around her neck and held on tightly. She waited until I had a firm, snug grip and then began to run across the frozen lake before sliding all the way from one side to the other. It felt like I was on a carnival ride, being transported back to my childish, free-spirited nature. She wanted a last dance with me before she entered the dreamtime.

My body started to shift into the body of a little girl around the age of six. I recognized myself when I was young. I remembered when my mother used to wax the wooden floor of the upstairs hallway between the bedrooms. My first dog Snoopy and I used to run from one side to another as we slid on the floor.

"Whee!" I yelled.

Tundra was going faster and faster. I could hardly catch my breath through all the laughter. This was exhilarating, I felt so free.

"Why are we doing this?" I asked, while giggling uncontrollably.

She said that I had forgotten how to laugh and how to have fun.

"Your life has become too serious," said the bear in a deep but compassionate tone. "You humans take everything so seriously and forget to play, so I am here to remind you of the importance of playing."

I was silent, swallowing the truth of her words when I noticed two familiar faces smiling at me, a man and a woman. They both had chocolate brown eyes and chiseled cheekbones. It was my dear, elder, Inuit guides, my guardians in the spirit world.

They were waiting for me on the left side of the lake. It was a long-awaited reunion. My eyes welled up and my heart softened. I let out a sigh of relief, it was so good to see them again. I always feel safe and protected in their presence.

They have been guiding and nurturing me since my very first trip to Greenland back in 1997 when they first appeared in a shamanic drum journey. They have never abandoned me and always turn up at the most perfect times.

Their appearance is always a sign of change, good change, the kind that pierces through stagnant energy. There had been too much of that lately. They come to me when I need to receive the next piece of the puzzle, the next clue for my life's journey. Their timing was impeccable.

The Universe is always giving us clues to assist us on our journey, but how many of us really listen?

I could just make out the igloo in the distance. It was half hidden, so I squinted my eyes to get a clearer look. The wind picked up and snow began moving in different directions as if it was twirling throughout the open space in a mystical dance.

My guardians reached out for my hands, one on each side as we made our way towards the igloo. Once inside, we sat down. Beneath my legs was a red and white knitted blanket. My motherly guide then extended her tiny, frail hand and put a morsel of fish into mine. This is something they always offer me during our meetings. I was honored to accept her offering.

The fish was delicious and felt so nourishing. It had a delicate texture, slightly salty and tasted like lake trout. The elders gazed into my eyes as I sat more comfortably, moving my bottom onto the warm blanket that insulated me from the icy floor. Our eyes bonded like magnets, more deeply than ever before. They began speaking to me in a gentle tone.

"You have forgotten to nurture yourself," they said. "You are so busy raising a family and serving others that you have not taken the time you need for yourself."

A tear rolled down from the corner of my eye, I understood their truth all too well and it shook something from deep within me as if I was awakening from a deep, hypnotic trance.

"It's time for you to write your next book," they explained.

I could feel the grief from deep within my being; I felt ashamed, I had abandoned my gift, my passion, my purpose. I could hardly catch my breath, trying to capture each moment as the years had passed by so quickly.

They nodded their heads, "You are now ready."

Their expressions changed to that of deep compassion and concern. I looked at both of them, trusting with the innocent eyes and vulnerable heart of a child. My body began to tremble as I released a long-awaited cry from deep within my soul.

"I trust you both, I really do, but you know how challenging my life has become with the juggling act and all the different hats I've been wearing over the years raising my children," I explained.

"I had no choice as I was completely losing my equilibrium."

"We understand, but it's time," said the woman I call my spirit mother.

My spirit father took my right hand and assured me that it would be okay. I let out a sigh and then gave him a smile; I was beginning to have faith once again. The wise woman smiled too, she then reached out to place a pouch around my neck for me to wear, a medicine bag. It was made of Arctic white wolf fur adorned with lilac suede. It was so beautiful.

"Here," she said. "Wear this for your new journey, it has everything you need, all the tools that will assist you on your new adventure."

I had no idea of what was inside of it, that would be kept a mystery for a while.

She looked into my eyes once more and placed both hands on my shoulders. I could sense her strong conviction that all would be well. I believed her, I truly did.

They both felt my trepidation and gave me a warm embrace. I breathed in deeply.

"Here we go again," I thought to myself. "I'd better hang on tight as it's going to be a wild ride!"

As I came out of the igloo, five wolves were waiting for me. One white, one black and the other three were grey timber wolves. They came to remind me that I am always looked after and that I am part of the pack. I then shapeshifted into a timber wolf myself and joined my pack on this new adventure.

We were now six, running so freely, leaving behind our tracks in the snow. A fresh flurry would soon cover them. I was home, back with my pack running wild and free; this was a reflection of my true spirit.

The beat of the drum called me back from my altered state. This deeply profound journey was coming to an end as the rhythm of my heartbeat slowed down. I was relaxed and grateful for another beautiful meeting with my spirit allies.

Many years had passed since I wrote my first book. I felt like a tornado had hit every part of my life. I now understood how important it was for me to go through all of the lessons. It made me wiser and stronger. I am able to better assist my clients and students having endured those years of challenges. More wisdom was acquired.

One thing I can certainly vouch for: this journey is no easy road! The path of the soul will shake you up, shred you to pieces and turn your world upside down. It doesn't have to be that way for everyone, but it certainly has been for me.

As for the soul seeker and searcher of absolute truth, you may have to enter a dark forest in order to find out more of who you are. You might also get lost amongst the trees as it can take some time to find your way back again. You may even enter into the darkest places where you would not wish to tread. However, the journey is not always dark. You will also encounter adventures that fill your soul with joy and absolute bliss, so do not get discouraged. Remember to reach out to others for assistance. There is always guidance available.

Are you willing to dive deeper into your being? Are you willing to swim in murky waters in order to reach the cascading waterfall? I had come so far and wasn't going to turn back around now. So, I decided to keep moving forward despite the diversions, distractions and challenges. I also witnessed many miracles. Pack light but fill your backpack with the things you will need to sustain you and get ready for a grand adventure.

## Wisdom from Tundra

Close your eyes and begin to breathe deeply. Feel yourself becoming more and more relaxed. Use your imagination and don't judge what you experience. This exercise is uniquely yours. There is no right or wrong way of doing it. Imagine you are meeting with Tundra, the playful polar bear. If you had a question to ask her about your life right now, what would it be? Be open to receiving whatever you may see, feel, hear or sense.

If Tundra had one word to show you, what would it be? You may want to write it down, sit with it, draw it or dance it out. Again, use your imagination to expand your creativity. What does this word mean to you at this particular time in your life?

Remember to give thanks to the spirit of Tundra and to your own inner wisdom and body. Gratitude changes everything and opens more doors into your creative and exciting life.

Always be gentle with yourself and know that you are constantly growing. You are not alone. Your guardians, spirit animals and allies are always with you.

## The Black Lone Wolf

I could see his amber eyes through the darkness of the cave. His nose began sniffing the cool, crisp air. My protector had appeared to me early in the morning, just as I had woken up but still partly in a dream state. He always nudges me not to run away from any problems I might be facing. Who would we be without having to face them? This is how we grow.

He prompts me to have courage and not let fear stop me from what I am truly meant to be. He is also a reminder to not be fooled by appearances. His glare is not scary, it is beautiful. The blaze in his eyes is that of my own reflection. We are sometimes afraid of our own reflection as it may be too powerful for us to truly understand.

Shadow, the black wolf, is another of my power animals. We all have a number of them guiding us. He was so excited to see me. He stayed by my right side as we began walking through a forest. The sky was grey, and the clouds were moving very quickly. I sensed that a storm was on the way. This was very symbolic for a storm was also raging inside of me. I was fighting something.

We all pass through storms, but when we surrender, it makes it easier instead of feeling like we are constantly battling. I was hanging on to the familiar, wanting to stay snug inside my den, but intuitively I knew it was time to come out and embrace what my spirit elders had told me.

Lightning started to strike, creating stunning artwork in the sky. My wolf was protecting me, shielding me from the wind that was picking up, and the downpour of driving rain that could have easily filled a bathtub. He moved even closer to comfort me. He is so affectionate and loving, I adore him. With him by my side I felt safe.

I've been meeting with Shadow for over thirty years now. He stands out and doesn't care about what others might think of him. He stands alone in his power and is so confident that not even this storm could knock him down.

It was getting darker now and I was having a hard time making my way through the trees in the darkness. Shadow sensed this and moved in front of me. I trusted him, so I followed his lead through the forest. The wind began howling, and for a brief moment I thought it was another wolf. At the same time, thunder crashed through the forest, startling me and shaking the earth.

We saw a dim light ahead through an opening at the end of the trail. Shadow guided me out into an open space, not shielded from the elements by any trees. I was curious and a little worried as to why he would expose us in this way. Shouldn't we be taking shelter somewhere within the forest? There was a lesson to be learned, to be felt, and he wanted to awake my intuition that had been asleep during this time in my life.

I watched as he began walking in circles while the lightning was striking all around us. He looked at me, signaling to join him in a secret dance that only he knew. With every strike of lightning, there was a sacred movement. I started to move my body as it became synchronized with each streak of light.

We were joining the earth's sacred dance. It was exhilarating and empowering. This was the dance that would change the course of my life. It was time to leave the comfort of my den, put on my shoes of courage, and start trekking the wilderness once again. My teachers were right, it was time.

## The Red Rocks Speak

I felt the spirit of the red rocks calling. I have always felt a deep connection to the spirits of the land in Arizona, especially Sedona. It calls to me when the time is right to visit. I remember my first visit to Arizona when I was twenty-nine. A friend and I were returning from a sacred Sundance in South Dakota we had been invited to attend. We spent several nights camped out at both the Grand Canyon and Monument Valley. It was pure magic. The presence of the red earth and rocks really captured something deep within my soul.

One evening while I was out walking through Monument Valley, I sensed the spirit of one of the rocks calling out to me. I stopped in my tracks, mesmerized by it. I felt a strong tug in my solar plexus, and I instinctively knew that something deeply profound was happening.

We travel to so many places as tourists but how often do we stop to acknowledge or to offer deep gratitude to the land and to the spirits? Every place has a memory, a soul. People visit certain spots for introspection, for inner peace or contemplation of their life.

I felt a deep sense of power within this rock. It was seeking my attention. I moved closer and put my hands on her; I could sense a woman's spirit. The more I connected to her, the more peace I felt within my being.

It was dusk, and although many people were out walking because it was mid-summer, it was as if it were just the two of us. You know those moments where you feel like the world has stopped everything just for you? I turned my head slightly to admire the setting sun. It was breathtaking, like a picture painted by angels. The sky was fire orange with melting streaks of gold. The air was still, and before long the valley of the Gods would come to life without another soul in sight to witness the wonder of their hidden secrets.

My attention came back to the stone. A woman's voice spoke to me softly. It was as if an angel was whispering to me from inside the rock. People assume they will only find angels by looking up at the sky, but they can be everywhere, even in rocks.

"Reawaken your soul," she whispered. "All things are sacred. To really appreciate the nature of all things is to know that everything is alive."

I pictured her having long, silky, black hair, dancing with every expression of the wind in an elegant movement. She wore an ebony and sapphire shawl draped over her shoulders that went just past her hips.

"If we were to walk as if every step was a prayer, life would be so different for all of us. If we paid more attention, we would know that everything has a spirit."

Still thinking about her words, "Is your spirit real," I asked curiously. "Can you explain more?"

"Your soul is ready to emerge in ways that you would never believe possible. Big changes are coming," she replied. "To stay open is to prepare for these shifts that will happen within and without your world as you perceive it. The spirit of many places will call to you. The spirits of the land are real, we are the stone people, and we are real."

I thanked her for the unexpected connection, honoring her, all of the other stones and the Native American people of the land for allowing us to visit and camp overnight.

Wherever you visit, always remember to thank the spirits of the land, and whenever possible make a sacred pilgrimage or ceremony. Your journey will be even more sacred.

That night it rained so hard, I had to put my towel over my head just to go to the washroom and even then, I still got drenched! There was thunder and lightning throughout night, which was another adventure and a powerful experience.

A howling wind had picked up making it quite mystical and also a little eerie, but I felt safe with the knowledge that the angel of the rock was protecting me. The weather didn't bother me. I was snug and warm inside my sleeping bag in my little tent. I felt shielded by a sapphire blue aura around me. I closed my eyes and drifted off.

## Through the Eyes of the Raven

The Raven has always been an important power animal for me, both in the spirit world and in the physical. Ravens with their jet-black eyes and blue-black feathers will give messages for those who wish to listen. The spirit of the raven has a certain zest for life, they are so very clever too.

Lessons can be learned just by observing them. I remember watching some as they rummaged through a Styrofoam cooler that was left at the campsite while some campers went hiking the Grand Canyon. It was actually quite humorous to me, but not so much for the campers on their return.

As I watched how strategic they were at going after what they wanted, it reminded me how sometimes people just sit back and wait for things to happen instead of actually going after them. If we pay attention to nature, it will gift us with an abundance of mystical teachings. What does the raven mean for you?

I remember another incident when I was visiting beautiful Crater Lake in Oregon with my dear friend Bruce. I was admiring the stunning scenery when two ravens caught my attention. A large male was on the ground while a smaller female was watching him from the branch of a tree. Suddenly she glides, here comes the other raven, making her way to him now.

This was a time in my life when I was a single mother. My ex-fiancé Andy and I were still friends but living separately in different countries. I was contemplating where my life was going and was unsure if we would someday get back together.

I continued to watch the two ravens as they took flight together, making their way to the top of a very tall tree. Suddenly a feather fell from the tree. It was as if they had dropped it just for me. It landed right in front of my feet.

My friend Bruce turned to me and said, "That was a sign, it is right in front of you, and you can't even see it."

I thought about Andy and our relationship. His love is right in front of me, and I can't even see it. That was the message from the spirit of the ravens. Not long after receiving that clear message, my son Keanu and I moved back to the UK so we could be with Andy. He helped me raise Keanu like he was his own son, and we soon got married and had two other children together. That goes to illustrate the awesome power of spirit.

Another quality of the raven is to remain a mystery and don't give all your secrets away. Some years back I had a very powerful dream where I was travelling through the eyes of a raven. Journeying through the eyes of the unknown was a profound place to be. Out of the void through nothingness comes clarity.

What messages does the raven hold for you right now? Imagine you are taking a journey to meet with the spirit of the raven. Use your imagination and let go of any judgement. Breathe deeply into your body, now free your mind and move into your creative visualization. Write down or draw the first thing you see, sense, hear or feel. Anything that connects to the raven. This is your personal message.

## Enter the Mystery

The place of the unknown. The void. The journey through the eyes of the raven. To see through blackness, the darkness lurking through the mist of the soul waiting for the sun to rise. It will rise into eternity. We merge into the mystery where the curious place of the unknown becomes the present. Being in the moment of time when the dark and light amalgamate into the presence of divine time. The place of contemplation.

Breaking through old patterns that were once the driving force of all things. Piercing through new life as beginnings take on a different form. Enter the mystery in all its invitation to re-explore the very things you once held close, but now hold behind in fear.

Dig deeper and enter your sacred temple. The mystery of all things that are divinely you. Into the unknown you shall find the deepest treasures of your soul. Mysterious you, divine you. When you choose to see, the deep divinity within will be revealed. You are the mystery; you are the gift. It is time to unveil the greatest secrets of your existence. Are you ready to explore further?

## Chapter Two

# Turquoise Healing

There are sacred lands with special healing powers dotted all across Arizona. It is also home to one of my favorite gemstones, the turquoise crystal. The therapeutic energy of turquoise can be felt throughout the red desert landscape. I am so grateful for the healing I have received over the years from the sacred lands I have been so privileged to walk on. I always remember to give thanks to the Native Americans whose land we are blessed to visit.

I have the fondest memories of all the family road trips we took through the Southwest when our children were younger. Those were such precious times that will stay with me forever.

I sat in my healing room and was guided to meditate. My gaze wandered to one of my favorite turquoise stones. I reached out and held it for the meditation. In my mind's eye, through creative visualization, I could see the pretty blue-green hues swirling throughout my being. I began to breathe deeply with them as they created a new kind of dance. The turquoise stone was beaming with calming energy and was assisting in bringing a deeper tranquility.

As I drifted further into an altered state, I felt soft fur brushing against my face. It was my white spirit wolf coming to comfort me. She was surrounded by a turquoise glow. The marvelous sight of turquoise light intertwined with white wolf fur was beautiful and soothing, guiding me into an even deeper state of serenity.

I started to see white and black feathers in the form of a headdress. I immediately knew who it was, my Native American chief guide who has been with me from the very beginning of my spiritual journey. He has been my guardian since I was born into this lifetime, although we have shared many others, and he will be my death guide when my physical body is ready to leave the earth.

He was my father in a previous lifetime and made a soul contract with me for this one. He understands the void I have felt, the yearning I've had since I was young, being raised as a fatherless child. I sometimes think I've carried my father's challenges with me since I was born.

It was now time to finally let go of that. I had been reconciling this, along with ancestral and generational healing for such a long time. All the years of being a shamanic practitioner had led me to this point. This was such a powerful healing opportunity that would help change patterns for future generations to come.

It is said there is always at least one healer in every family, although I truly believe we are all healers in some form or another. I could no longer carry this burden, it was time to release it. As I continued to heal, so too did the soul of my father and of my ancestors. I always know when my chief is with me as I can see the very specific feathers of his headdress and feel his powerful presence. He gets straight to the point and doesn't tolerate any small talk.

"It's time to put your shoulders back," he said reassuringly, as he began pulling out a dark energy from my upper back. It was a blockage of sadness that I had carried for most of my life.

"Breathe deeply," he continued, as I exhaled this deeply rooted sorrow that was finally ready to leave my body. I had carried it for long enough. I had learned so much from it, even befriending this heartache, just to hold on to something associated with my father, who sadly, I never really got to know. It was time to be free.

As I continued to breathe out, I felt like a heavy burden had finally left me. There was now an empty space inside waiting to be filled with a new positive energy. My chief placed the most beautiful turquoise stone in that area between my shoulders. I could feel its healing power moving throughout my body and then into my heart.

"You can put the sorrow to rest now," he said softly, "you have healed. Stand tall and be the woman you were meant to be. Express and expand your creativity. As you do so, others will also expand into their own uniqueness. You are all here to assist one another. Like a pebble that you throw out to the ocean, it skips and jumps, leaps and bounds, and so will all of you."

He continued, "Your soul pod is expanding. People throughout the world are all finding one another to inspire and create. Our world is changing. The earth is healing and will continue to heal. People are being strategically placed in all the right areas to reconnect. A meeting of old souls is rising. Like-minded, lighthearted people are coming together from all over the globe to help make this world a brighter place for future generations. But we must reawaken the sleeping soul within."

As I became more relaxed, I saw myself entering a turquoise cave. It was breathtaking, powerful and gentle all at the same time. I looked around in awe of this miraculous wonder. The walls were a gorgeous blend of teal and cyan. It was incredibly magical. I found myself a place to sit down still mesmerized by this cave.

My chief had now disappeared, but I heard a different whisper, this time from a man speaking Italian, although very faint. I could feel a presence beside my left shoulder. It was my father; his spirit had come to visit me. He was so real, as if he was in human form once more.

"I am connected to your chief," he told me, "I always come through with him."

I could no longer see any of the feathers, but I intuitively felt both of their spirits with me.

My father, who served in the navy, told me he was now

liberated and so very happy, "I am the free spirit I once was, when on a boat. That was my happy place."

Perhaps that's why I love the ocean so much.

He told me, "It's time to let me go, to finally release me and make peace with the life of suffering I endured. You are ready for your next chapter."

He took hold of my hand, lifted it up to his lips and gave it a gentle kiss.

I was alone in the cave, feeling much gratitude for my life.

## Meditation in the Turquoise Cave

Immerse yourself into the healing energy of the turquoise stone. If you have access to one, hold it in your hands or just keep it close to you. Be still and visualize yourself in a cave filled with the most gorgeous, turquoise energy. Be present and bring yourself into a more relaxed state.

Be aware of all your senses. Invite the powerful healing spirit of turquoise to uplift you and bring an inner calm into your being. This is a great stone if you feel exhausted. Release anything you may be aware of that is weighing you down. Let go of the burden and allow the turquoise energy to transform it.

As always, spread thanks throughout your whole body. Breathe in the gratitude and continue to sit quietly until you are ready to emerge from the cave. Listen to your intuition. No one knows better than you do.

## Journey of the Heart

The will of fate and destiny plays its part. Your whole life is a journey deep within the heart. When we are in alignment with our heart and soul, everything comes to life. The stuck becomes unstuck. This is where true movement happens. Sometimes you must lift yourself out of stagnant energy, the head space we get bogged down in, and dance your way back to your heart so you may express yourself through the song of your soul.

## Walker Between the Worlds

You are free. It is a time of transition. No more wandering. Time, purpose and travel all intertwined into the deeper depths of being. Transcendence is interwoven through the inner dance and the cycle of birth and death.

This is a good transition but it's very important to be present, recognizing the stopping points. Between time and space, sometimes altering perception of reality. Shift the flow and go into a new direction. Walk a new path. Break the pattern of the stagnant energy.

You are a master of destiny. You have the power to walk a different direction that will revitalize your soul. Acknowledge where you are and be honest with yourself. If you want change, then you must be conscious and in alignment with your full feelings. This means being fully present so you won't miss what is right in front of you.

## In the Dreamtime

"The journey is not complete, finish the journey," Lia's voice echoed through my mind, merging with the sound of the drumbeat. My body felt relaxed as I drifted into each beat until I found myself back in a familiar place. My bare feet were planted firmly on the red earth. I could feel the heat from the scorching sun radiating out from the ground, warming my soles. I took a deep breath and inhaled the atmosphere.

"I am here, child," she called, then once more. "I'm here, child," her voice growing louder, the softness fading.

There she was, sitting on the edge of a large rock. She greeted me with a smile; I noticed the space between her front teeth. My old friend had returned. I smiled back at her, beaming with joy. Her hair had silvery grey curls, hiding what remained of the black hair beneath. It was maybe a hint of a shade whiter than the last time I saw her. She wore a red skirt that hung past her knees, and a pretty yellow top complemented with white flowers.

She opened her arms, and I immediately ran into her warm embrace. Lia took my hand as we began walking toward the cave. I felt nervous.

"She is taking me to see the old sorceress," I thought to myself, and took a deep gulp while clearing my throat. A wave of apprehension washed over me as I remembered how intimidating these meetings with her could be.

"Just don't look straight into her eyes," I reminded myself.

She is here to help me and not to frighten me, but even so, it would still be an intense meeting. It felt wonderful being back in Australia, even if it was for just a short time and through altered reality. I looked down at the path we were treading and saw three small, brown snakes leading the way into the red rock cave. I had already overcome my fear of snakes, but instinctively knew they were not here to harm us anyhow. The snakes suddenly disappeared, and I saw a shaft of light coming from the entrance.

"It's not dark in there anymore," I thought to myself. It appeared more illuminated and not so intimidating. I could feel the presence of the old sorceress. Kauala was her name.

She called out to me, "Come, come closer."

"Kauala's voice sounds frail," I murmured to myself.

"Sorry, you are not frail," I quickly corrected myself as I recalled she could read my thoughts. "I don't think she would like that very much."

I moved further inside and there she was, sitting by the wall of the cave. Her silhouette was slightly illuminated by a shaft of light coming through a small crack, but the rest of her still shadowed by the pitch darkness behind her. I briefly glanced at her face, remembering not to stare directly into her eyes.

Her hair was a little longer now, still a fluorescent white, slightly wavy with stringy ends that draped across her ribcage. She wore an earthy brown shawl wrapped around her tiny body. Hanging from her neck I noticed her large, rectangular selenite pendant with a round malachite stone embedded into the center.

"Don't mistake age with weakness," she murmured, "and don't mistake growing old for growing weak! You know, one grows wiser and stronger. Looks can be deceiving and many people are coming in different disguises for you on this new journey. Beware of the ones that will run you down. Remember, the owl is always there for you and knows deception very well. There will be no deceit this time. You see, child, it all comes back in the circle. Everything is bringing you back to the circle of oneness, but you forgot to complete one last task."

Although fully present within the altered state of this journey, back in my own reality I could hear an owl in the forest behind my room where my physical body lay drumming. It was hooting and grew louder and louder. Synchronicity at its best, and another validation for the seeker.

"So, what is this task, wise one?" I asked.

She handed me a crystal sphere. I could see all the prisms and rainbows inside of it. She told me to place it on my brow chakra. My third eye instantly became a beacon of light shining through this crystal ball. I could see all of the eons of years, colors and journeys of my soul. Everywhere that my essence had travelled. Each of the colors representing a different era of time.

All the chakras in my body were spinning, vibrating, illuminating and accelerating. It felt like an initiation into some kind of rebirth and renewal, a celebration ceremony happening deep within my body. The old sorceress handed me a pen. It was royal purple merging into magenta, with yellow gold at either end, and three diamond-shaped moonstones around the top. It was stunning and vibrant.

"This is for your new journey," she announced. "This is to remind you of all the support you have along the way. You are never walking alone, even though at times in your life you have felt abandoned. Your guardians always walk with you. Remember this," she explained. "This is no ordinary pen; it really does have magical powers! It's like a chameleon that changes with each vibration and frequency that you enter."

She continued, "You write your own reality and create your own story the way you want your life to be, but now that you have let yourself know your soul more deeply, it is illuminating. It has set off a radiance for others around the world. Many will come to you from different parts of the globe because you have important information for them. They can then empower themselves and create their own stories."

I could feel my body really spinning into a higher frequency. I opened my eyes for a moment to bring myself slightly out of this intense journey. I was looking for an exit sign, for a way out.

"Don't be frightened, child," she said softly, "you will always be grounded. Don't be afraid of the higher frequencies, you have done the work thus far, now you are ready for the next part of your journey. Go into the direction where your heart tells you to, it will never steer you the wrong way, and always ask for guidance."

"But where am I going, Kauala, and what do you want me to do?" I asked with sincere curiosity.

"You have many pathways, child," she replied. "Many roads that will take you to different places in the world. The earth's energies are shifting and changing, we must start helping to bring balance to the world once again."

The spinning sensation came over me once again.

"That's right, you keep breathing," she encouraged. "As long as you have the breath of life, you have the breath of brilliance, the breath of continuum and continuity. Another veil has lifted. Go, go out of the cave now and Lia will come for you."

She smiled and looked into my eyes. I was no longer scared to return her gaze. I felt empowered, protected and filled with immense gratitude for another encounter.

"Thank you, wise teacher," I exclaimed, "I thought you had forgotten me."

"I don't forget any of my children," she replied. "We are all sacred children of the earth and you have come back into this time to remember who you are. I am from forever, but you see you are from forever too."

"What is forever?" I asked.

"Forever is eternity," she replied. "There is no end to existence, you have come from the place of forever just as many of the people who will come to you and learn with you to fulfill their purpose. It's time for all of the children of forever to speak their truth."

I reached out my hands to join with hers. I saw a bright light going through me like electricity, energizing and revitalizing my spirit. It was making way for my soul to navigate the next part of the journey. Her hands integrate into mine, we become one energy. I am her and she is me, she is a part of all of us.

As I stepped out of the cave, I noticed it was now illuminated even more, filled with so much light and love. The radiance was glowing. It felt just like the aurora borealis. I looked down at my feet and placed them firmly on the earth with clear intention on this new journey ahead. My soles felt hot now in contrast to the cool dampness of the cave floor, as the sun was beaming even brighter.

Lia was there waiting for me. She took my right hand and walked me back to where we first met. The path through the red rocks and the color of the sand had now changed. It had turned a brighter, more vibrant red, with swirls and patterns of black and rust. She led me over to a Lia tree where all of the beautiful flowers were in blossom.

"You must complete this book by spring," she said sternly.

"The circle will be completed, and you will see all the blossoms. Your first book was not complete and cannot be complete until the second book has been written. It is a continuation and the two will merge into one."

"Where do I start, where do I start, Lia?" I asked.

"Start by stepping back into the circle," she replied. "Remember?"

"Yes, I do remember," I told her. "There is something different about you, Lia."

"I thought the same of you, child," she said with a smile. "I think we both look a little brighter."

"Yes, I think so too," I replied.

She kissed my forehead and wiped the dust from my third eye.

"Do you remember the stone I told you about?" she asked. "The one that you dream with. You need to go back to that stone, the dreamer's stone, and it will help you to create this book. The sun is always guiding you, look at the sunset, look at those beautiful colors."

Neither of us could resist staring at the magnificent sunset. We stopped talking for a moment to marvel at this masterpiece and capture the beauty of the mystical, orange, purple and red colors illuminating the sky.

"The spirit of the moon will soon be visible," said Lia, "but for now, let's enjoy this very moment of the here and now."

"I give thanks to our Earth Mother, the spirit of this land," I said. "I pay tribute to you and all of your ancestors. Thank you for not forgetting me, Lia. Thank you with all of my heart."

I felt like a little part of myself had returned, the girl who somehow, somewhere, lost her compass for a while. Living life with all the responsibilities and juggling my duties in the best way I could. Being a mother, wife and serving clients and students from around the world. There needed to be a balance, and I eventually had to slow things down in order to respect my process, my mind, body and spirit. Life is not always easy, but I can see how I got lost in it all.

We need to honor where we are, and no matter what, come back to ourselves. Heal and forgive without abandonment even through chaos, heartbreak and confusion. It's all in the lessons that will turn into blessings if we can have a new perspective. Returning to self is the key.

This is a time for rebirth and renewal. If you are being called to make changes in your own life, now is the time to dig even deeper, to discover who you really are. You are a gift. Take in a breath of new energy, new life. Welcome a new vitality, open yourself up to divine guidance and know that the journey always continues.

## Wisdom from Kauala

If the old, wise woman in the cave had a gift for you, what would it be?

Close your eyes and begin breathing deeply. Feel yourself becoming more and more relaxed. Use your imagination and don't judge what you experience. This is uniquely yours. There is no right or wrong way to do this exercise. Imagine that you are having your own brief encounter with Kauala. She hands you the gift. How does it make you feel? Is there any meaning behind it?

You may sometimes get a clear answer, or you may want to explore this later and come back to it. Always remember to give thanks. Fill yourself up with gratitude.

# Chapter Three

# Becoming Autumn

A time of mystery, a time of maturity, a time to welcome the season with wonder. Breathe in the crisp Autumn air. Sit with me a while. I will whisper to you the secrets of this mystical time of year. Sip on a warm drink and watch as I begin my journey of liberation. The magnificent array of colors as the leaves begin their journey of transformation.

## Autumn Mist

Curious to me, I feel lured by your mystery. Revealing just a little at a time, exposing the mountains but not the full view. The mosaic of colors is magical, yet the darkness through clouds of haze is alluring. Is there something more you want to reveal? Am I not yet ready to see the mysterious unveiling?

The leaves fall, removing the illusion of hanging on. The brume remains while I continue to grasp so tightly. The mist starts to dance in the sky with its message to let go.

If you want to see the autumn sunset, surrender. Sometimes it is harder to hang on. Release or you might miss the crimson sky. The autumn mist is your friend. Do not run from the haze. Do not look away for that is when the mystery will be revealed.

## The Dancing Leaves

Their splendid colors from green to yellow, orange to red and gold, what a joy to see them dance so graciously in their expression of true freedom as they let go. Their graceful release in their glorious artistic movements. Outside my window they begin to fly as they ride the gentle wind.

In their excitement, they come to show me how liberating it is to let go, swirling in divine movements before offering themselves back to the earth. They waited for this release just so they could have their last twirl.

Watch me, you might want to even catch me as I fall from grace in the divine dance of Autumn. You too may learn to let go, it's not as hard as you think. It can be a great dance of salvation. I have so much to teach you. Come and frolic with me. Soon winter will come.

Don't miss this magical portal of the great liberation. I have matured through to this stage and am now ready for the next part of my journey. It will be a fun dance if you just release with me. Come on, it's your turn now.

## Tonto Monument

Just when I thought I had already healed so much over the years, I entered a portal of opportunity. This was a predestined day, as everything fell into place with so many powerful opportunities for healing. This was a gateway forward to acceptance, and also a bringer of many hidden gifts. The blessings would show up many years later. I could not believe the level of extraction that happened.

I was told in a journey to come to this place as it had something to offer me. I have been practicing the shamanic arts for over thirty years, and have built up so much trust with my spirit guides that I know to listen to the guidance that comes through. If it feels right, and I am able, then I will graciously follow it.

I didn't know at the time what to expect apart from what I had read. This was a journey of deep empowerment. My dear friend Jolynn was in Arizona at the time, so I invited her to come join me.

Jolynn has been like a soul sister to me, a kindred spirit who has shared many joyous adventures with me in Arizona, and especially in Sedona. She has been on her own spiritual journey for over fifty years, and makes beautiful bundles of sacred holistic medicines from sweet grass, sage, lavender and other powerful healing herbs.

The drive to get there from Phoenix was gorgeous and very scenic. We drove through the beautiful Superstition Mountains, passing Apache Lake, and then into the Tonto National Forest.

We parked the car and began our ascent. Walking up the steep trail to the monument was slightly challenging, but the view was incredible overlooking the pristine blue water of Roosevelt Lake.

We were surrounded by the cactus gods, both male and female. The cactuses were everywhere! Agave, Jumping Cholla, Prickly Pear and Giant Saguaro. Every cactus is a protector; they are the guardians of this sacred cliff dwelling. They are very much alive and carry many stories. If only they could have told us about the Salado culture who were believed to have been a group of wayfaring Anasazi, living here comfortably between 1150 and 1450 AD, prospering from their artistic skills with ceramics and the weaving of cotton fabrics.

We could feel how the ancestors awakened with excitement upon our arrival. Jolynn and I had such a powerful healing experience in this sacred place. We could feel the shifts happening within us even as we walked through the cactus trail. The sun was beaming in all the perfect places, and also gave us shade at the exact times we needed it. This made our experience even more mystical.

The prism rays radiating through the sunlight were incredible with vibrant, magical colors. Jolynn and I experienced so many healing extractions here, not only from previous lifetimes, but from this one too. It was happening in such a profound way that my visualization was at its peak.

As we sat down to rest and admire the magnificent scenery, aquamarine light filled my body, rejuvenating all of my cells to the core of my being. This mysterious place had magical healing powers. As I connected more deeply with the sun, purple, white and golden rays expanded through me. I felt as if I was receiving a spontaneous reiki healing session and began thinking of my beautiful, kind and gentle reiki master, Therese.

She had transitioned many years ago in her eighties. Since her passing, I've had several dreams of her playing her crystal bowl over my body, helping to balance my chakras. I believe our loved ones can still send us blessings and healings from the astral realm. You just need to believe and be open to receiving.

That was one lesson that was hard for me. It took me such a long time to be able to receive. I had spent most of my life mainly giving until I reached a burnout stage and realized that my body, mind and spirit needed to be more open to receiving. That is when my life started to turn around.

There needs to be a balance in your flow of energy through both giving and receiving. Do you find yourself mostly on one side or the other? If so, try bringing balance to your flow of energy.

This will bring about changes in your own life.

We continued to follow the steep path to the upper cliff dwellings and ancient cave. This was such a profoundly powerful place, both Jolynn and I could feel the spirits all around us. We stopped to offer some sweet grass in honor and gratitude to the spirits of this land.

I could sense the blessings of my two native spirit guides. They have walked with me since the beginning of my life's journey. On my right side, I could feel the feathers of the elder man's headdress as they softly caressed my face and shoulders. On my left, the younger man's long black hair was blowing gently in the breeze. I always know when there is an important event or when I am entering a place with high vibrational energy as these two master guides will always show up. They like to remain a mystery, both mystics, who I am so blessed found their way into my life.

Take a moment to pause and breathe, and then try to tune into who is guiding you at this very moment. You may have a sense, or a feeling, or be already aware of a deep connection. They may have shown themselves to you in a dream. Respect their presence and always ask why they have come to you. The more you quiet the mind chatter, the more you will feel the connection.

You can do this with creative visualization, meditation or by taking a shamanic journey. My very first shamanic journey forever transformed my life. I would not be the person I am today. It hasn't been an easy road, but it's been a very rewarding one.

I believe the whole process of life is about relinquishing and shedding. This is how we grow. It was the perfect time of year, and my favorite season, autumn, when the leaves fall so freely and naturally. They don't fight to hang on, they just surrender and dance to the melody of the wind with such grace.

We finally made it inside the cave. This was another place of deep healing. I could not believe the level of extraction here. There was a lot of letting go. The spirit of the turquoise energy was so therapeutic, as I continued to release all that no longer served me.

As we moved further inside the cave, I felt a little dizzy as my energy centers started to activate and realign back into balance. Like everything in life, there needs to be balance. As a mother, wife and teacher with amazing students and clients, I know how crucial this is. Being a super sensitive soul, it is so easy for me to take on too much and lose balance. It took me quite some years to learn the art of letting go. I am still learning how to shed and balance my life. My three children are growing so quickly that I want to cherish each moment I spend with them.

The word 'forgiveness' kept running through my mind. I breathed into the word to try and understand more deeply. This was about forgiving myself, being so hard on myself and having all these expectations. My heart was heavy; I felt as if a gush of water was pushing against a dam that finally broke. I began to sob uncontrollably in a powerful release I could only imagine had been welled up within my body for such a long time.

I have carried so much over the years, but we can only process as much as our mind, body and spirit can take. The trauma I have experienced was beginning to show up in different ways in my body. My hair was thinning, and I was reaching perimenopause. Big changes were happening within my body. My marriage had also become very challenging; it was a confusing time. I had healed so much on this journey, but how many more layers could I shed?

My psyche was ready to bring forward many things that I could not remember throughout my childhood. Our physical body is our greatest gift, but we often take it for granted. It carries secrets and stores all the memories within it. It is your greatest teacher and will always let you know when something isn't right. It is also wise enough to know when you are ready to face the past. It is so important to pay attention to how your body is speaking to you.

As memories started to come back, I surrendered and started to become even more present in my body to allow them to be grounded. As painful as the experiences had been, this was the only way to move forward. I embraced all aspects of myself without judgement.

Healing trauma is not an easy path, but when you set up a support system and are willing to move through it with acceptance and grace, you will become unstuck and see a new path opening. We are all unique, on our individual path, so everyone's healing journey will be different. Only you know what will work for you, and when the time is right. For myself, it has been an ongoing, lifelong journey, and I continue to heal as I remember more of the forgotten trauma. The more I remember, the more I return to my true, authentic self.

I recommend you seek guidance from a great counsellor, therapist or practitioner so you don't have to go through this alone. Sometimes your loved ones can offer assistance too, and then there are always your wonderful allies in the spirit world who are loving and supportive. I give thanks every day for the guides that walk beside me.

Jolynn and I continued to meditate in the cave; there were no other visitors at that time, so we were able to deeply connect with the spirits. We gave thanks for the healing we had received and held a gratitude ceremony in honor of the essence of the land, and the long-forgotten Salado people that once lived here, before vanishing without a trace from this secret and mysterious place. Traces of their existence remain hidden under the red earth and in the spirit of this gloriously landscaped land.

We both felt a sense of tremendous renewal. Just as our ceremony ended, other tourists started to arrive. We were once again blessed by divine timing. As we were leaving the cave I caught a glimpse of a white spirit horse in the distance. I intuitively knew this was an introduction to her wild energy that would one day lead me to another portal. On our way back to the car, Jolynn and I were rewarded with the most magnificent, fiery sunset. We were both beaming with an aura of love and gratitude.

## A New Equilibrium ~ The Gateway to Your Sacred Ceremony

If you could gift yourself with a sacred ceremony, what would that look like? Who would you want there with you? What would you bring: flowers, herbs, objects, memories, music, art, an instrument? Gather all the things that symbolize this journey for you. If you could call on a spirit animal for this occasion, who would come to join you? If you have not yet connected with one of your power animals, you can take a drum journey or meditation or even have a blank paper in front of you and just draw the first animal that comes forward. Be creative and remember to expand your imagination. That is the key.

## Harvest Moon

Soon the snow will fall gently on these dwellings and the memories will become more vivid through dreams. The harvest moon brings messages of stillness and peace, of a life that was once lived in this ancient place. It has preserved a spot within the pocket of my soul. I entered the home of this bygone land that calls to me on this autumn eve. The echoes of the past in this mysterious place bring a light of peace, new beginnings and understanding, as I watch the dragonfly enter along with the echoes of our ancestors.

A white spirit horse comes to greet me. We head to the narrow pathway, as the aura of the moon lights up the trail and illuminates the darker places within my soul. Home to memories once lost that want to reveal themselves through that brief time between autumn and winter, where the seasons change, and the soul engages in a much brighter journey of fulfilment.

## Ancient Healing Well

The next day, Jolynn and I were called to go to go to Montezuma Castle Monument. We had heard of the amazing healing that some have experienced at the well. We were still feeling revitalized from the amazing experience we had at Tonto National Monument.

We arrived at the well after our walk through the incredible scenery of the castle. I found myself a comfortable spot and began to pay my respects to the spirits of the land and to the well. I felt peaceful and began to meditate.

During my meditation, I kept seeing and hearing the word "gifts". I breathed into the word and intuitively connected with the energy that was being presented. I moved into my creative visualization, the place where I expand my imagination but also align with my intuition.

Then I saw a beautifully woven basket. It was cream colored with accents of pale red and light blue, and diamond-shaped designs around the outside. It really was quite magnificent, and was filled with carrots, turnips, parsnips, pumpkin, squash and corn. It represented a time of harvest and Thanksgiving. A time of abundance.

I was guided to go deeper into my own belief system about abundance. This is something that I have always had to work hard at because of my own upbringing. I grew up in government housing, raised by a single mother of five. I often wonder how she coped and managed to raise us all by herself. Somehow she made it through on her own arduous journey.

I now have three wonderful children of my own, and it certainly hasn't been easy for my husband and I. Being so far away from family and not having that extra support has meant relying on each other for absolutely everything, causing a lot of strain on our marriage. My mother did the best that she could. I am so grateful and blessed that we made it through those difficult times. I now understand how tough that must have been for her.

It was also hard for me, feeling like I was different from the other children. I always felt like the poor kid from the hood. Especially in elementary school where most of my friends had two parents and lived outside of the government housing system. I often felt ashamed and not good enough. This caused me low self-worth throughout my early years, something I've had to work at terribly hard to overcome. It has been a struggle for me to embrace abundance.

The great Bob Proctor taught me so much about how to shift paradigms and how crucial it is to change your mindset. He has helped me to feel comfortable with abundance, which now happens to be one of my favorite words.

I struggled a lot at school, but was not fully aware at the time that my learning ability was limited because of dyslexia. As I grew into adulthood, I began to understand how differently my brain comprehended things. Once I embraced my neurodivergence, I realized how truly abundant I really was, in more ways than I could have ever imagined.

When I saw all of the lovely gifts in the basket, I could really relate to the feeling of abundance because I was open to receiving all of them and more. But just as fast as my basket was being filled, it began emptying again, and then a moment later it refilled itself. At first, I couldn't understand why that was. Then the word 'gifts' reappeared, and I heard a whisper, "The spirits will keep refilling your basket when you share your gifts with others."

This was starting to make sense to me now. We are all here to share our gifts with one another. It was so rewarding to see the basket being filled, then emptied, then refilled again. There was no end to this cycle, and the energy it was creating was truly euphoric. Abundance in all good things is here for us all.

When we are ready to receive and truly believe that we deserve all the goodness in the world, it will come. I know this because I've lived it and have done so much work on shifting those inner paradigms. When you journey through your interior and do the work necessary to progress, your exterior world begins to change. You then create your own reality, the life that you truly desire.

I began to feel deeply connected with the land and was aware of how wondrous nature really is.

As I came out of my meditation, I could hear the spirits of the land talking to me. I reached for my journal and pen, and asked what other words of wisdom they had for me to share. Below are the messages that I received. You may wish to pause for a moment and think about what these mean to you.

- Walk this earth in a sacred manner.
- Clear any negative energies.
- Be careful who you share your energy with, making sure your values align.

- Embrace your individuality.
- Explore and expand your creativity.
- Honor yourself and others.
- Love yourself and your body.

All of a sudden, there was a light rain shower. I looked up with my palms opened wide and welcomed this gift from the heavens. It was so refreshing and felt appropriate as the cool raindrops gently cleansed my face. It was a perfect moment of blessings from the spirits of the well. The journey was now complete. I felt a profound sense of renewal, deep within my soul.

# Part II

# Integration

# Chapter Four

# Reflections of You

The rain is falling on this autumn day, creating tiny ripples in the puddle where I stand. As I look down at my boots, I catch my own reflection. I watch more closely as these dancing circles quickly vanish, then reappear with each new raindrop. You are poetry in creation at its finest hour. You are a mystery waiting to be unveiled, a gift wanting to be opened. You are creation in all its splendor, an unlimited being throughout time and space. You are timelessness.

Will you honor this reflection of who you are?

## Amber Eyed Woman

She is ancient, she meets me at the crystal clear waterfall. She breathes fire into me, life force back inside of me where I have depleted my own vitality. Life has been weighing me down, my whole being is exhausted. I've been carrying too many burdens and responsibilities of the world.

"Why do I carry so much?" I ask myself. "It is not for me to carry this debt. Is it really my birthright to carry the weight of my parents?"

It is said that it only takes one person per generation, down the ancestral line, to break a paradigm. But this is the pilgrimage of my life, seeking to fully understand my soul's journey. We are all protagonists in our own stories. We have the opportunity to create a life with purpose.

"Why do I have to feel so deeply?" I often ask myself.

I am a super sensitive, neurotypical woman who sees and feels so very much. Sometimes the huge burden on my shoulders is too much to carry by myself. My ancestors watch me, knowing I have chosen this path to liberate not only my soul, but that of my parents and their predecessors, through deep generational healing. Too much is outdated and expired, there is too much baggage for me to carry. I need to put it all down and rest for a while.

A few years ago, I was fortunate to take part in a musical and spiritual pilgrimage through southern Italy with Alessandra Belloni. I will never forget the incredible, spontaneous healing that took place in a small town near Benevento, just outside of Naples. It was here that I would finally release the burden I had carried for fifty-two years of my life when I came face-to-face with the Black Madonna of Moiano.

Our group was allowed to go into the church and sit with her. When it was my turn to see her and offer a prayer of gratitude, I couldn't believe how beautiful she was. Her eyes pierced right through my own with a level of love and compassion that was simply indescribable; I have no words.

My whole body started trembling. I became very emotional, while a miraculous healing took place. It was in this sacred little church in the region of Campania that I would fully surrender and leave behind not only all the baggage, but all the curses that were put on my parents too. In the old Italian ways, the evil eye or what was known as malocchio in ancient times.

It was believed through whispers that this curse had been placed on their marriage and even carried on beyond. What I didn't realize was the huge impact this has had on me throughout my entire life. I was so grateful for the life-altering experience and to sit with the stunning Virgin Mary, Our Lady of Freedom. It was finally time to free myself and my family from the effects of the curse.

Are you conscious of any burdens you might be carrying from your ancestral lineage? If you feel called, invoke the spirit of Our Lady of Freedom, and pray for her guidance and assistance. Stay open to the miracles and the healing. This can be very profound.

Amber eyed woman is waiting patiently at the cascading waterfall. I have met with her during my meditations for over twenty-five years. She is a small, elder lady in her nineties. She is of frail appearance but this must not be mistaken for weakness. If you are not careful, just one look into her hypnotic, fiery eyes might put you under her spell. She has long arms for her height, and her white hair stands out against her copper-colored skin.

Our meetings are usually brief, but straight to the point. She has been guiding me through my spiritual journey of truth. She offers courage, strength and stamina to help fulfill whatever mission you are out to complete. Amber Woman looks into the eyes and straight through the soul.

There is no escaping her gaze. Any old beliefs that no longer serve will escape into her withering hands as she captures and destroys them violently, right in front of your very eyes. She will swallow them with no mercy, setting fire to every last shred. Be ready to part with anything that is outdated, running you down or chaining you to a pitiful life. The fire in her eyes will draw out any remaining self-imposed pity or lack of self-worth as she has no time for false values or tantrums you may be clinging onto. She will extract any last remaining fragment that has held you prisoner in your very own self-contained cell of despair.

Be prepared, for if you dare meet with her, you'll be taking a very clear look at your own reflection. The truth about who and what you truly are, without any masks or disguises. This journey is one of courage and is not for the fainthearted but can be ever so rewarding.

Are you ready to embark on your own inner pilgrimage? Are you ready to meet with her and look at your clear reflection as it mirrors through the flames in her fiery eyes, the flames of truth? As your soul reflects back at you, it reminds you of what you carry deep within your own heart, showing you where you may have abandoned your very essence. Amber Woman has no patience for self-pity. We have all been there at some point in our lives, but she appears like a phoenix to assist when you are ready to rise from the ashes of the flame of your soul.

The sound of the thunderous, yet somehow soothing waterfall becomes clearer. Behind the mystical curtain of cascading water, I can make out the silhouette of her tiny body. As I walk toward her, I catch a glimpse of her burning eyes watching me approach.

She comes out from her hiding spot and is now visible through a gap in the canyon walls. This time she has a walking stick made from chestnut. Her shadow can be seen seeping out between the red rocks.

She greets me with a half-smile, as her eyes begin to lock with mine. I look away, glancing down at her feet. Surprisingly they are young and fresh looking, as if she was still a teenager. Not at all like the feet of an ancient wise woman who has graced the earth for centuries. Her hair is thick and straight with wisps of white and grey complementing the remaining black. She is wearing an emerald green dress, cut off at the top, exposing her shoulders. Around her neck is an oval-shaped amber stone the size of a mandarin.

She doesn't speak spoken words, but she will communicate enough wisdom telepathically, straight into your heart. A dazzling flash of light, captured from the sun's rays, is reflected through the amber stone that sits over her heart. It gives me the courage to return her gaze.

"I come to liberate and empower you," her eyes inform me, softly but sternly.

"Thank you," I answered.

"Reach out and touch my amber pendant. Feel the vibrant energy radiating through your hands," she said with her mind.

As I grasped the stone I could feel the heat radiating from it, and saw amber energy being transferred into my hands. It began pulsing through every part of my body until my whole aura looked like the amber stone.

"That's it," she said telepathically, "now feel the vibration as it reenergizes and revitalizes you."

As I closed my eyes, I imagined myself inside a giant amber crystal. I felt confident, powerful and protected.

Her eyes spoke to me one last time. "Now you are ready for rebirth," they said.

If you have the courage to call upon the spirit of Amber Woman, what personal message would her eyes have for you?

## Through the Eyes of an Owl

I can see through you, right through your own deception. You may have been deceived by others, but there is no greater deception than self-deceit. To go against what your own intuition tells you, instead looking for answers and approval through other people. No one knows your truth better than yourself. The answers you are seeking are already inside of you. Master self-knowledge and you will master your life.

Look into my eyes and see the mirror of self-reflection. Why do some people fear me? They think that I come to show death, but it is the death of the old self needed for rebirth. What old ways do you want to shed? Which old habits or patterns are keeping you stuck? Do you wish to stay trapped through fear of the unknown?

I come to assist you in finding your strength from deep within. Once you are empowered, you can move into the right decisions that are aligned for you. If only people would stop running from me. They are really fleeing from themselves, their own power, their own light. That is what they are afraid of.

I am also here to help you grieve. Let go of the sadness from the life you thought was meant for you, and allow this new life to work itself through you. Stop thinking you can control everything. Loosen your grip, why is it so firm?

I tell things the way they are. I show the truth and some can't handle that. I can see through the darkness. Some people are so used to being in their own shadow, they lose sight of what is important. Once you have embraced the darkness, will you be willing to move out of it?

I come to share my wisdom. Are you ready to hear it and see clearly?

## The Distorted Mirror

You look into the mirror to reflect back at yourself. Is it truly you or a distorted image of yourself, painted through life's challenges? In moments of despair, you become something other than your soul. You grasp onto something in order to define yourself. What are you defining? Who are you truly becoming? You will be whatever your experiences in society have shaped you to be.

It is time to look at what has caused this false reflection. Some people don't even realize when their own image gets distorted. Look beyond what your shadow shows of you. Look through your eyes more deeply to where the mystery has been hidden, unveil it.

Look closely at your true reflection and you shall be taken on a grand adventure. This is all about your perception of yourself and how that influences your life. How you see yourself is how others will view you too. How much longer will you go on deceiving yourself? Polish your mirror so you can have a clearer view of who you really are.

## The White Lone Wolf

My loyal white wolf reappears every time I have allowed someone to deceive me, or even deceived myself. She reminds me of my truth and dissolves everything that is false. I step out of the cave, it's cold here and I am no longer wanting to stay. I am alone. I have been lonely for such a long time and yearn for my pack.

She-wolf has carried her burdens across the frontier, through thunderstorms and winter blizzards, in sunshine and in rain. The suit of armor that protected her for so many years is ready to be removed. She trusted no one but now she has the courage to walk out of her den.

She howls out into the naked cold, brittle air. The reflection of her breath can be seen in the morning dew. She shakes off any remains of the heaviness she once carried. It is finally gone. The armor hits the ground like a lightning bolt. Generations upon generations of wolf packs.

Here she stands with her call for her wildness, to return to the pack she so desperately seeks. Her head held high in pride, she sings her glorious arrival across the barren landscape. Her howls echo through the atmosphere, the wide-open wilderness. Every breath of rawness touching the terrain.

The white wolf begins her pilgrimage to recover her pack.

## Whispers in the Wind

As humans we put so many limitations in our lives. It is our mind that does this, limiting us until the great wind of freedom breezes over us. It reminds us that we are free spirits and we have come here to be liberated, to be joyful, and to bless one another on our journeys.

We are all kindred spirits, wandering, searching and seeking. We are trying to unveil the deepest mysteries of the unknown. Surrender and it will bless you with divine grace. Let go of the abstract that keeps you from your true potential.

The wandering soul seeks adventure. Move into the flow of your natural rhythm and you will experience all that life has to offer. As like-minded beings, we nudge one another, look for the signs. Sometimes it's a gentle call and other times it is a fierce roar, reminding us of our sacred journey. Don't get trapped or wrapped up in the chaos of life without seeing the natural beauty. Continue to be free flowing in your own natural rhythm so you can hear the whispers in the wind.

## A Choir of Wolves

Out on the great landscape of eternity, the four wolves are waiting for her. The task is done. Her time of introspection is complete. They await a new journey, for the next new adventure across the horizon onto new terrain, creating fresh memories.

The pack has rejoiced in her return, their warm welcome of howls sounds like a great choir, divinely orchestrated by the Universe. The new moon begins to rise above the canyon walls just as the sun retires from a long and glorious day. They jump on each other showing great love and affection, gently nibbling the faces and grooming one another. Their hearts beat as one.

At long last, she is home. They begin their quest across new, rugged lands, taking them even further than the last adventure. She is feeling stronger than she has ever known. Her stamina is restored.

Fluffy snowflakes begin to fall, gently covering the ground in a thick blanket. A flash of green and a tint of red northern lights decorate the night sky. We make fresh tracks in the snow, as a new story begins.

# Chapter Five

# In and Out of Altered States

When you tap deeply into the energy of Sedona, it can have you moving into altered states of awareness. There is an opportunity for transformation at every vortex that you visit. Even during the drive to Sedona, you can feel your awareness shifting.

About an hour away, I started to feel the land nudging me. The experience of being connected to the earth's energies from this magical place is incredibly empowering. The high potency of the vortexes offers an entry point through every portal.

Be aware of each gateway you are entering with clear intention, even if it is just to offer gratitude. This helps you remain in alignment with the beautiful energies. Stay in your heart with your feet firmly planted on the earth. This will help you balance your equilibrium while connecting to higher frequencies. The support of mother earth will help to ground you.

The vortexes offer healing, serenity, balance and personal empowerment if that is what you are seeking. Pay attention to the land, the wind and the rocks as you enter through higher vibrations. Everyone's experience will be different, dependent on their own personal, unique transformation.

## Entering Sedona

I can always feel the energies and where my body is aligned before I even arrive in Sedona. This is an indication for me to tap into the frequency I am currently holding so that when I return home, I will know how much has shifted in my vibration. If my timing is right, the first place I visit upon entering Sedona is the Chapel of the Holy Cross, to sit quietly, say a prayer and light a candle. This is also a ritual where I set my intentions for the time I have there.

The chapel was built in 1956 and stands tall between two natural rock pinnacles. This is one of Sedona's beautiful vortexes and one of my favorite places to visit. The most cherished memory for me was when I visited with my whole family including my dear mother, Carmela.

My mother taught me at a young age to respect the spirit of the saints and to pray. It was such a blessed day I spent here with her, my children and husband, one I will never forget.

My mother would often pray for over five hours a day, but never for herself, always for others. During my travels throughout the world, wherever possible I would make sure to get my mother a new rosary from a sacred sanctuary or church. I may not have been a practicing Catholic throughout my whole life, like my mother, but my connection to the Creator, angels and saints has never left me. I have a deep love for them as I do for my precious mother.

If you visit this sacred place, expect to feel a sense of inspiration, love and joy. Lighting a candle in the sanctuary will also bring deep inner peace. I like to remember all those dear loved ones that have passed into the spirit world. I always feel them close to me when I am there.

## Airport Mesa ~ The Masculine Vortex

Another year had passed since I was last in Sedona. She was calling once again, only this time it was in the spring. The sacred land always calls me back when it is time. I usually get the nudge to go in the Autumn, but the messages from my beloved Inuit teachers and Lia were echoing through my soul. I visualized the pen that Kauala had given to me and the sacred pouch my spirit parents gifted me. I remembered how they told me it would help on my journey.

The signs and synchronicities to write my second book were upon me. I knew this wasn't going to be an easy task with my dyslexia, as it takes me a lot longer to write and to structure a book.

However, it is my passion and purpose to use the gifts of my imagination to help others on their journeys, so of course I would honor it. My spirit allies have never let me down. I love and trust them with all my heart. I just needed to stay open for the guidance even if at times it didn't make total sense. Eventually all the pieces of the puzzle always come together.

After visiting the Chapel of the Holy Cross, my next stop, just in time for sunset, was the Airport Mesa, also known as the Masculine Vortex. With one of the best views in Sedona it is a wonderful place to spend the evening admiring Arizona's fabulous sunsets, and I highly recommend this as a place to visit if you come here. It is a good idea to arrive a little early during peak season as parking can be limited. After traversing the short but fairly steep trail to the top of the Mesa you will be rewarded with the most spectacular panoramic views of the valley and rock formations below.

It is said that the energy here can assist in activating your chakras along with giving you a greater spiritual perspective on your life. With a 360-degree view of the surrounding area, some people believe it is the one place where you can absorb the full energy of Sedona.

This is a great vortex for reenergizing your body and boosting your self-confidence and self-worth. It strengthens the masculine side within, bringing a balance to those who tend to have a stronger feminine side. I always find it extremely empowering just to visit, even more so when I meditate here. It is a great place to contemplate how to take full control over your life and make the right decisions.

Another of my favorite memories is coming here with my whole family during a road trip. Our children were younger, and you could see how energized they were by this vortex. We loved our road trips across the Southwest and have such wonderful memories of visiting here on so many occasions over the years.

We would always try our best to arrive here for sunset. Not only are the views particularly breathtaking, but it is also a little cooler in the evening. It was always a grand adventure, and our kids loved clambering over the rocks.

I was getting ready to head back to my hotel for the night, and started planning what I would do the following day. There were still many people watching and waiting for that precise moment to capture the perfect photograph. I was just thinking about visiting the Feminine Vortex when I spotted two lizards, one to my right and one to my left. To me this represented the two aspects of the psyche, the masculine and the feminine, and the balancing of these two different energies.

"How perfect is that?" I thought.

What will you let go of today? What no longer serves its purpose? It's all about enjoying the journey, so why are we always in such a hurry to get to our destination?

A way will always be made, a pathway will always open for you. Just breathe and go with the flow.

## The Dreaming Lizards

As I headed down the trail towards my car, I caught a glimpse of the two lizards once again. They reminded me of my spiritual journey, my dedication as I continue to walk between the worlds. It was also a great sign for regeneration and rebirth. This could not have been more in alignment with where I was in my life.

Tap into the energy of the male vortex and call upon the spirit of the lizard for deep dreaming and a more fervent activation of your intuition. There are many different spiritual definitions for the lizard. It symbolizes dreaming, regeneration, rebirth, power, protection and strength. In Australian Aboriginal culture, lizards are part of the dreaming stories related to the creation of the natural world and our ancestors.

The important thing is to ask what it means for you personally during this time. Close your eyes and draw in a deep breath. Imagine you are in a peaceful setting somewhere in nature. Quiet the mind chatter by focusing on your breathing. Let go of any stress and tap into your imagination, your creative visualization.

Imagine you can see a lizard. If nothing comes to you right away, don't worry, don't judge yourself. Stay with the feelings of tranquility. If you could imagine a lizard, what would it look like? Be aware of what you are sensing, feeling and seeing. Trust that whatever comes through to you is relevant.

If the lizard could speak to you today, what would it say? Give thanks to the spirit of the lizard. Take in another deep breath and bring yourself back. Focus on fully grounding yourself with your feet firmly planted into the earth. You may choose to draw a picture of your lizard with colored pencils or even paint it. This will help to strengthen the connection.

Be sure to write down your experiences as you may wish to reflect on them another time. You might just be amazed by the messages waiting for you when you come back to them at the most perfect time. I have been logging my meditations and journeys for over thirty years. I have discovered deeply profound wisdom hidden inside my journals when I refer back to them, and my books have been written through this very process.

## Journey from the Heart

"Come back to the dreamtime, child," I could hear the old sorceress whisper.

I found myself travelling back to the cave where she was waiting for me.

"You have journeyed well, walking on different parts of this world, placing your hands and feet with care and gratitude into the earth's desire for deeper understanding. Mother earth is grateful for your endearment and great honoring of these sacred lands," she explained. "You and your fellow humans must continue to heal the planet with love, eliminating hatred from your minds, your mouths and your actions. You must create a more peaceful world for future generations." As she continued to speak, her tone became softer and gentler. I sensed a kind heart, her words streaming straight from her soul. I witnessed another side of Kauala, her voice now serene like gentle rain falling on a hot summer's day. It was so refreshing, she opened my heart.

I could see where I had been holding back in my own life, where I could've been more peaceful with myself and others. What if the words we spoke to one another were like a clear and tranquil, free-flowing waterfall? What if we were to thank the earth every day and honor every part of nature we are so blessed to explore?

"Come look at this," she said, while grabbing my right hand tightly.

I noticed her moonstone ring, it looked just like the one I was gifted by my students while in Sedona. It is my favorite ring. I also noticed how beautiful her hands were, so elegant with a road map of lines representing all her wisdom throughout time.

"Embrace the years as you earn and gain the wisdom of life," she said serenely. "It is a great honor to see another day. Each morning when the sun rises you are truly blessed. Just as the stars illuminate the night sky, so should your heart light up your body, the sacred temple within."

Her eyes opened wide and she spoke straight to my heart as she looked through the window of my soul. "You must keep your heart open, keep compassion and love moving unconditionally. With every disappointment you have closed it a little more. You must allow the stream of serenity to flow through in its own rhythm. Stay within the flow of consciousness, don't allow the actions of others, society or the news of our world to harden your heart."

She pointed to a small opening in the wall of the cave, "Look at what you see, this is the miracle of life for all humanity. This is nature's gift with all its splendid colors. Will you embrace life's beauty, or will you dwell in the darkness of this cave? It is for you to choose. All the children of this world have a choice how to look at life. No matter what the circumstances may be, your mind will always dictate your future. We have been gifted all the colors of the world, we must embrace the beauty that lies within each and every one of us, as we merge all the colors of humanity into one."

I looked through the opening in the wall, a window where I witnessed the most incredible sky. It was truly miraculous. There were no clouds and I could see a rainbow extending from the red earth right up to the stars. It seemed so close I could almost touch it. I was mesmerized, in complete admiration of the vast array of colors. It really was the most magnificent rainbow I have ever seen. It was a spirit rainbow, a gift from the cosmos.

I drew a deep breath to take in the full essence of this majestic display.

Kauala continued, "Keep breathing deeply and expand all of these colors through every part of your essence. You humans have become so comfortable sitting with your darkness that you are afraid of your own light. It's time for all humanity to embrace their own luminescence and expand it across the world into the collective consciousness. That is what our planet needs right now, for everyone to rise up from the darkness into the light. This is how to bring about peace, through the expansion of the light. It will spread so quickly, ensuring the eternal flame of existence keeps burning."

I froze in silence as her truth cut right through anything else I may have been thinking. Her words were sharp and pierced through any remaining darkness I had in my aura. I could visualize a candle burning deep within my belly, spreading the flame from my interior, allowing it to radiate through my exterior presence. Her wisdom began to warm my shivering body as I knew this all too well. It was as if she had wrapped me in a blanket of truth to comfort me and stop the trembling.

Many of us, including myself, find it so hard to embrace our light, our brilliance and beauty. It has taken me so many years and I have come such a long way, but I will always be a student on this mystical journey. I know how much my own life and the lives of my students and clients have been transformed, when we are willing to do the work that is required. It never really does end. It is perpetually ongoing, but the miracles to be witnessed are worth all of the effort.

"Now look into my eyes," she commanded.

I remembered how scary it was to look directly at her, so I hesitated.

"You are being reluctant, second-guessing yourself," she said. "Don't you trust me? Or maybe it is yourself you don't trust. Think about that for a moment, then when you are ready, look at me.

This time with complete faith and trust."

I thought about why I was so nervous of looking deeply into her eyes. Was I afraid of myself? She was right, we are so scared of our own power, our light, that it prevents us from moving forward. This is the place where we get stuck.

Pause for a moment and think of how you have stopped yourself from making progress. Are you stuck in your own life? If so, in what area? What could you do today to take a step forward into embracing your light?

I was ready, I had mustered up the courage now as I wanted to continue progressing along this life journey. I looked into her eyes, they were a deep dark brown. All of a sudden, they turned crystal blue. It was a gateway, and I knew that something was about to shift as I moved into a deeper meditative state.

Her agate blue eyes transformed into a tunnel that I started travelling through. The tunnel led me through the window where I could see the entrance into the rainbow. I saw that my feet were firmly gripping the red earth. It felt like they were getting ready to take off like a rocket. My body could feel the energy from all the vibrant colors of the rainbow inviting me in. I was ready to bathe in all the dynamic colors.

I held my arms up to the sky, and took a step forward. I had entered the rainbow ray. It was incredibly healing. I started moving my body into a dance. The colors of the rainbow were orchestrating my movements as I was swirling through each color in a sacred dance of oneness. Being in this light was so euphoric.

"Why are we so afraid of it?" I thought.

I was still in a trance dance. The rainbow was so incredibly bright, I could barely make out the celestial sky, lit up with a thousand stars. The moon had now woken up from its deep slumber to complement the blanket of stars. I was now bathing in silvery moonlight, while watching the stars wink at me.

"This is what happens when you embrace your light, the essence of the universe enlivens within you," Kauala explained.

I could feel the blessings of the rainbow moonstone ring she was wearing. It was supporting my inner growth, giving me strength but also enhancing my creativity and intuition. I stood in the glow of the moon and felt enchanted by the magic of the night sky. I understood how important it was to embrace the light and have the confidence to move forward in my life without being influenced by what others think about me.

We are not fully aware how different our lives would look if we just let go of the judgements of others. I was ready to do just that. I felt the calling of my dear teacher and quickly travelled back through the tunnel of her powerful blue eyes. I thanked her for another lesson and for all the guidance she offers.

During my meditation I must have fallen into a deeper state

of consciousness. I was laying in my bed, but I felt like I just ran a marathon. I was ready for a restful sleep.

## Rainbow Blessings

Take a moment to write down some words of wisdom about your own life. What did you learn from Kauala? If you were to step out of your darkness and embrace the light, what would that look like for you? Now take a moment to imagine that you are standing at the root of the rainbow. Your feet are deeply connected to mother earth and your body is expanding through all of the amazing colors. What clarity comes from this? If you feel called, you may want to draw or paint the colors of the rainbow and your experience for deeper connection.

Now bask in the night sky with the moon and the stars blessing you. The Universe has a personal message for you. The message could be long or just one word. Maybe an image, a feeling or even a song. Don't judge, everything is relevant. Breathe it in and expand your light and beauty out into the world. Continue to radiate from the inside out, and remember to embrace your light.

# Chapter Six

# Cathedral Rock ~ The Feminine Vortex

This portal has a very gentle, soothing but powerful, magnetic energy. It is divine grace of love and beauty. This is one of the most awe-inspiring vortexes to be photographed, with the natural beauty of the red rocks standing so proud and bold amongst the picturesque healing waters of Oak Creek. This is my most treasured spot to meditate in all of Sedona.

Her energy is audacious. She is not afraid to embrace her femininity for she is one with herself. Her feet are firmly grounded. She is earthed. Like all the other vortexes, enter this one with purpose. A crystal-clear intention will heighten your experience here. This is a great place for cleansing and renewal. To enter the great womb of the mother is to enter the ocean of oneness with no limitations, so come as you are.

Everyone's encounter will be different. The flowing creek, so abundant, cuts through any stagnant energy as it magnetizes your soul's experience. This is the one vortex I could never skip, as I always witness the reflections through my own cycle of life here.

The journey of life presents us with many things. At times the edges are rough and jagged, other times they are soft, smooth and silky. It is how you respond and interpret the things that are coming into your life that makes the difference.

I encourage you to perform a gratitude ceremony here. This can be as simple as just giving thanks to the spirit of the land, or you may want to design your own more elaborate ceremony. As you flow with the spirit of the creek, remember the cycle of life, and how its rough edges can be polished, opening a clearer path for you to tread. Fill yourself up with the love and light that will radiate through to the outer world. Let the sunshine into your being and continue to flow into your own natural rhythm.

Remember that you do not walk this journey alone. You are to be used as an instrument of divine grace while the gentle breeze blows through each one of us. Remember your blessings and let go of expectations and outcomes. Breathe in life, let it in. Help will always manifest when you are stuck, but there will be distractions so stay on course. Inhale love and gratitude.

I give deep thanks for the spirit of the land, to the people who came before us, to the spirit of Oak Creek, and to the keepers of this divine vortex that offers us so much in its generosity. I give thanks for my life and all that I have, for my husband and our beautiful three children.

What are you grateful for? A thankful heart changes so much in your life. Again, recognize and break through any stagnant energy. This is a great place to help you to move forward and get back into the flow of your life. Remember that distractions will always be around to challenge you, it's just a part of life. It is all about moving through the situations with grace; you must always trust your journey. Let go of any expectations and outcomes. Don't let anyone distract your inner serenity. There are always lessons to be learned.

As I breathe in the magic of this vortex, I dip my bare feet into the creek, splash my face with the refreshing cool water and begin to meditate. I see an image of a stunningly, beautiful woman who looks like a Goddess. She is wearing a white gown and is playing the harp. She has long, chestnut hair past her waist, and wolf-like hazel eyes.

"My name is Dignity," she tells me.

The elegance in her delicate hands and long fingers represent her divinity.

"You have no idea how happy that name makes me feel," I reply, "I have waited a long time to be in this vibration."

As I look at her, I see golden rays of sunlight passing throughout her whole body, appearing to be her aura. Her smile brings through a deeper calm. It washes over me, passing through my being. I sat still in her stream of serenity until I felt fully rejuvenated.

Your unique Goddess will appear to you in her own unique way at the divine time. The purpose of her connection with you is to bring more tranquility into your life. Whether you are visiting here physically or just connecting spiritually to this vortex, open yourself up to the blessings she has to offer. Feel the magic that she brings to you. Breathe into the essence of her spirit and feel the healing energy of Oak Creek. See yourself becoming revitalized and refreshed by the sacred water.

This is your unique ceremony, a date with your soul. You can sense the enchanting music entering your heart chakra as you hear her playing the harp. It uplifts your energy and empowers you, reminding you who you truly are. Have you forgotten the very core of your being?

Surrender and move into this gentle, yet high frequency. Your intuition will guide you as to how long you will stay connected to her energy. Remember, once the connection is made, you can revisit her and this place anytime either in person or in your meditations and soul travels. Once the healing is complete, you will see her going back into the water.

I will never forget my initial encounter with her spirit. She first visited me when I brought my daughter Amethyst here for a soul blessing before her first birthday. That was the same day my youngest son Aragorn fell into the creek and my husband Andy had to jump in to rescue him. He was only two years old and didn't know how to swim, but somehow his head stayed above the water, even though it was carrying him downstream. His older brother Keanu and I were reassuring him that he would be alright, and that his father would quickly swim to his rescue. I intuitively knew it was the Goddess protecting him, holding his head out of the water until his father had reached him and brought him safely back to shore. We all had a cleansing ritual on that powerful day. It was also a reminder to always take care around nature even somewhere as beautiful as this.

Remember not to judge what you experience. This is your own unique journey of tranquility. Pay tribute to all the blessings that come to you. Stay in the flow of your own natural rhythm as you connect more deeply to this vortex and the abundant energies of Oak Creek.

## The Mermaid Cave

Some years later, during an acupuncture session, I drifted into a meditation and found myself at the Feminine Vortex once again. This time I was met by my beautiful and dear soul sister, Cher Lyn. Her soul has always been in the heart of Sedona. It can be felt even stronger now after her transition into the spirit world. She was an incredible visionary artist and guided others on sacred tours to the faery wheel and medicine wheel.

My husband Andy and I were so fortunate that she blessed us in a sacred faery, water ceremony many years ago in the healing waters of Sedona. Cher Lyn was a very special soul with the gentlest energy, and I loved her dearly. She brought so much joy to everyone she met. Every meeting with her was profoundly inspirational and healing.

Her stunning artwork and card decks can be found all over Sedona, especially in the ChocolaTree. A magical, inspirational place to eat healthy, organic, high-energy, vegetarian food. This is another portal where many synchronicities can take place along with meeting kindred spirits.

I found myself at the point where I can feel the highest energy, it is where the creek flows fiercely from the entrance point of the Cathedral Rock portal. I sat down to rest in my favorite spot. As I gazed at the surface of the water, I could see Cher Lyn's reflection. She looked angelic, like an image of light coming through the water. From the waist up, she was radiating an aqua blue aura.

She called out to me softly, "It's me."

She swam closer to where I was sitting. I turned my head toward her and saw that she was a mermaid. Her torso was aqua blue, blending into a pale peach tail from the waist down. My dear friend was now in the image of half angel and half mermaid. Her energy was radiant. She was swimming in the water with shimmering rainbow lights moving through her. She looked almost translucent at times.

"Come join me," she invited.

It looked like a portal into another realm. A spiraling vortex of water was moving in a clockwise direction like a whirlpool. The colors were soothing. I had a feeling I've never experienced before. I was calm, but also curious, and I trusted my friend so I jumped in to join her. We admired the scenery together, soaking in the beauty of the autumn wonderland, with subtle blends of red, orange and yellow shades merging with the backdrop of the red rocks and pink sky. It was stunning, it truly was.

We swam beneath the surface where she showed me an underwater cave. I could make out the image of another mermaid guarding the entrance. She was the gatekeeper, perhaps the mother of all mermaids that lived here. She glared at me deeply as if scanning my whole body. Her bright blue eyes were sharp and hypnotizing; I tried not to gaze at her for too long. Her hair was bright yellow, her torso strong and solid.

Cher Lyn looked tiny there next to her. The water had changed into a more turquoise color; I felt like I was now entering an ocean. The mermaid gestured at me with her eyes as if granting me permission to enter the cave. I followed my dear friend inside as we swam even deeper.

I looked down at my own body as I started to transform into a mermaid myself. It was so easy to swim with my new tail, and I could now breathe under the water; I felt so liberated.

I could see all kinds of pretty colored fish, yellow, blue and red, swimming all around us. Cher Lyn took my hand and my body began swirling around as we swam in a circular motion together, dancing in liberation. She was finally free.

I felt so honored to have been invited to visit this magical place. The salt water was healing every part of my body. There were magical powers in this ocean of transformation.

She had brought me here to liberate my mind and for me to experience a new kind of freedom. I knew she was in a place of ecstatic joy, a place where she was able to continue her creative, healing work. She had painted her new life and it was euphoric.

## The Talking Mermaid

We were now communicating in a different way. It was our minds that were speaking, a special kind of telepathy. A unique way of talking in every sense. It was at a higher vibration, a brand new language.

"Don't take things too seriously," she said, "let certain things go that are not worth keeping in your mind and body."

"I wish I could take this new light body back with me once I'm out of the meditation," I thought. It was glorious, a truly liberating experience.

We continued to swim through to the deeper depths of the ocean. On the seabed was an antique jewelry box, a little treasure. It was golden with a pattern of geometric shapes that somehow reminded me of a lotus flower. Cher Lyn handed it to me so I could see what was inside. As I lifted the lid, I could see a shiny colorful shell. It was a gorgeous mother of pearl. It was a gift from her soul to mine. I was under the ocean, but I felt like exploding in my own wave of tears. I was deeply moved by this sacred gift. She looked straight through my eyes and our souls recognized a love through to eternity.

I held the shell in my hands, brought it up to my chest and thanked her through my eyes and my heart. She felt my love and gratitude, and I felt her love for me and for all of life. She is a part of everything. Her love is everywhere.

She quickly led me back through the cave and to my meditation spot. I could no longer see her, and came back to the red earth where I was sitting. I could hear the tranquil sound of the creek. I gave thanks to the spirit of the creek and the land at Cathedral Rock. I opened my eyes just as my acupuncture session was finished. I grounded myself and sat up in the chair.

## Meditation at the Feminine Vortex

Begin to breathe deeply. Connect to the energy of the Feminine Vortex once again. Be aware of what your mind, body and spirit are now feeling. Flow with the natural rhythm of the creek.

Listen to the sound of the running water and be aware of anything else nature has to offer you at this moment. Visualize that you are bathing your feet in the refreshing cool water. Feel yourself becoming rejuvenated by its sacred healing powers. You may also want to dip your hands.

Remember to thank the spirit of the creek. How do your hands and feet feel? Go ahead and cleanse your face now, paying special attention to your forehead to bless your third eye. Sit here for a while until you feel the tranquility move through you.

You may hear the whispers from the mermaids, or even an invitation to join them in the cave. Use your imagination to guide you further into the vision and listen for the sounds of nature as they will speak to you more clearly.

You have now entered a new portal, a place of endless possibilities. This is a gentle place where you will feel nurtured. Allow your visions and dreams to come forward as you feel the support from this divine threshold, and focus on your deepest desires and intentions.

## Mystic Meadow

Vibrant colors of purple, green and yellow merge into my heart, capturing the deepest desires as the swirling vortex of creativity sparks a deeper flame from within. Magical beings dance joyfully in the meadow with dragonfly wings radiating through sunbeams. Ladybugs gather on leaves playing a happy game together. Bluebells are blossoming beside the mossy green walkway.

My inner child is waking from a long winter's sleep. Come take my hand, let's frolic through the mystic meadow of timelessness. All the children emerge from hibernation, gathering for a celebration. The birds hear our laughter and rejoice in a great flight of freedom and liberation.

## The Songbirds

On my walk back through the forest, I spotted a gorgeous yellow cardinal. It began singing, and so I stopped to watch and listen. I felt like it was singing its song just for me, what a precious gift. After the incredible experience I had down by the creek, this was surely the icing on the cake. Another cardinal came to join it, a red one. This was such a beautiful sight.

Cardinals represent good luck and manifestation. I took this as a sign, one of great encouragement for writing this book. I also took it as a blessing from above that my departed loved ones were with me on this journey.

It brought me so much joy to hear their sweet love songs, and to watch them communicating by chirping, and looking at each other in the eyes. As I was admiring their bright colors against the green backdrop of the meadow, the red cardinal reminded me of the base chakra and the yellow one represented the solar plexus.

They flew closer, landing on the branches of a tree, the yellow bird to my right side, and the red bird to my left. This was the first time I had seen cardinals. Life is so beautiful and exquisite with so many of nature's wonders. I continued to watch them, the red bird appeared to be male, and the yellow one looked like a female.

This was another reminder of the divine masculine and

divine feminine energies, and how wonderful it is when there is a perfect balance between the two, along with admiring their own individuality. In nature, they are always parallel, in balance and in harmony with one another.

This is a great message for all of us. They were at different sides of a tree and yet they are kindred spirits, soul mates.

To my surprise and delight, a much smaller yellow-and-grey-colored cardinal came to join them; it was their baby! This was such a miraculous sight, watching this young bird climbing its way up the branch toward them. As I looked on in admiration of these stunning birds, the female began to feed the baby as the red bird watched over them.

I felt a deep connection with the souls of the mother and father and the miracle they had created. Life truly is a wonder to behold. Just then, the three birds started singing in unison. I leaned against one of the trees while being serenaded by their sweet melody.

These true gifts from nature don't need to be told who they are. They never question how or when to sing, they just flow with nature. They open their little beaks, let their magical songs ring out to the world and will never be silenced.

The yellow bird landed even closer to me, reminding me to sing my own song and use my voice. Just close enough, then she flew off to another branch. If we could just remind ourselves how closely connected we are to everyone and everything, it would change the way we live our lives. Each of us singing our songs in unison every day, no matter what life brings us.

## The Old Man in the Tree

It is just before dusk as I am leaving the Feminine Vortex. I notice the sun's rays shining through the gaps between a tree's branches where the moss has not gathered. I can feel the aura of the tree pulling me closer, so I step off the trail to my left where it is standing. I look at the tree more closely and reach out my hand to connect with its energy. As I breathe into my imagination, I see the image of an elderly Japanese man.

He resembles an older version of a spirit guide that I first connected with years ago when I initially began journeying. This guide only visits me on special occasions, maybe a handful of times each year. He has long white hair parted in the center, covering his eyes, and a long white beard covering his whole body, the only parts of him protruding, his knees and his arms. He appears slightly tilted as he peeks out of the tree at me.

He has manifested as the spirit of the tree and they feel intrinsically connected. He shows me an entrance in the trunk, a power spot that has blue light radiating out of it. It seems to be emanating from a turquoise stone that has been placed there. As he leans forward, his beard parts slightly in the middle, and I see the same turquoise energy coming out through his naval. I can now also see his left eye piercing out at me from underneath his hair, and notice he is carrying a samurai sword. The handle is sapphire blue with intricate pink cherry blossoms and gilded around the edges.

I ask permission from the tree spirit if I may stand with it for a while. There are branches projecting out from the roots and I cannot find a comfortable place to sit. I can hear the gushing waters of Oak Creek flowing so powerfully in the background. He is happy for me to stay and the energy feels inviting. I feel the gratitude from the spirit of the tree too.

Do you ever sit or stand with trees? This can be a powerful and healing experience. The Japanese practice of shinrin-yoku, or forest bathing, is becoming more common around the world, as people are reporting wellness benefits such as rejuvenation and reduced stress. It's a wonderful practice that brings more inner peace and serenity.

I put my hands on the tree trunk. The tree feels old, and yet somehow softness against my palms. The spirit of the old man comes through more clearly.

"I travel through many dimensions, places where many dare not tread," he explains.

"What lessons can others learn from your teachings," I ask, "and what is your message for us?"

"I teach infinite wisdom," he replies. "This wisdom is accessible to everyone, but there are few who are brave enough to go there."

I can hear birds singing all around us.

"Take a step back and have a really good look at this tree," he tells me. "I want you to see my purpose. Within me is an old spiraling tree with new baby branches coming out from the roots. This is where you are right now in your life. Most of us are like babies wandering in new worlds, discovering new territories."

I look down at the support from the earth underneath my feet. It reminds me to stay grounded and earthed as I am travelling through these journeys and meditative states. It is important to keep your feet on the ground without getting carried off into the ethers. Mother nature will always support the journeys we walk but it is imperative to look after our earth mother.

I study the various branches, some are large and thick, some smaller and thinner. Some appear old and rugged, and others are shiny and new.

I now glance above the branches and notice the sun trying to penetrate the thick clouds. It reminds me that we will have some bright days where the sun is radiant and other days where it remains cloudy. On those days, we must honor the clouds, honor how we are feeling and sit with it. We must not run away, not every day is meant to be filled with radiant light. There is so much to learn when we surrender into our body. Be still and ask your body how it is feeling. Deeply connect to the wisdom of your sacred temple.

This tree is also a sacred temple. The old sage is the guardian of the tree. He rests here in all of nature's joy, and speaks to all those who come to visit if they are willing to hear. You will find him nestled somewhere in the Feminine Vortex at Red Rock Crossing.

"Do you have any last wisdom?" I ask.

"Be aware of your comfort zone," he says. "Don't get too cozy in it. Be flexible, this journey is one of wonder, so enjoy every step."

Behind him lies the mystery and the secrets of where he once travelled. I see people's names carved into the back of the tree, showing where they have once travelled too.

I suddenly sneeze and then bless myself. It is not arrogant to bless yourself, so be sure to do this every day. I hug the tree and thank its spirit and the old sage, knowing he would reconnect with me again. There was more wisdom to come.

# Chapter Seven

# Star Spirit Tree

I woke up to a gorgeous, sunny spring day. It was a perfect day to hike to Kachina Woman at the Boynton Canyon vortex. When visiting this vortex, you will want to allow for more time, not only for exploring and hiking, but also to sit and meditate. It can be one of the most exhilarating experiences.

As I set out along the trail, the energy of one of the juniper trees began calling out to me. I could feel its spirit inviting me to go and sit with it for a while. I put down my backpack and made myself comfortable. There were a few other people sitting by some rocks close by, but they were getting ready to leave.

You will always find fellow kindred spirits in Sedona. I have made lifelong friends here. It is so wonderful to make conversation with all the like-minded people, and to hear their amazing stories of how Sedona has inspired them and changed their lives, especially from visiting the vortexes.

I could feel my solar plexus pulsating. I looked up to see a beautiful Christmas ornament hanging from one of the spiraling branches. It was a golden star representing divine oneness for all humanity. That is what it meant to me. I could feel myself becoming more relaxed and began meditating.

The vortex energy of the juniper tree had spirit animals inside of it. The wolf, lynx and fox were coming to me through the energy of the tree. I could also feel the spirit of an owl. Next a cougar came forward. It was as if the tree was shapeshifting into the qualities of these spirit animals. Many lessons are here for us to learn from the animal kingdom.

A raven hid behind the tree trunk and then poked his head out and showed himself. He brought me an egg. It was golden and the size of my palm. I wasn't sure of the purpose of this egg or what it meant, but I graciously accepted it.

The raven was bringing new eyes to me, teaching me how to see through the illusion of life. I didn't quite understand this. I started to move into a deeper meditation with the spirit of the tree and all the power animals that had shown up.

I immediately reached for my lilac spirit pouch with the white wolf fur that my dear Inuit teachers gifted to me. I felt the presence of their spirits coming closer. I could feel their warm embrace. Oddly, it was as if I had been transported back to the Arctic, even though in reality I was in the middle of the hot, red rock landscape of Arizona.

They raised up my hands so I could get a closer look at the pouch. I could feel their love and guidance, their hands intertwining with mine as I stroked the soft white wolf fur.

I remembered how sad I felt being in a store a few days prior, where they had three full white wolf furs hanging up beside some timber wolf skins. The shopkeeper had to get me some tissues while I sobbed for the spirit of all those wolves that had been hunted, most likely for sport. My heart had been completely broken and shattered into so many pieces.

I spoke to the spirit of each wolf that had been killed, apologizing for what had happened. I honored their spirits and told them they mattered, that they meant everything to me. I knew their spirit was with me, acknowledging their magnificence and divine beauty as I continued to stroke the fur, with each tear continuing to fall from my weary eyes.

It was so hard for me to break away from them. I felt like I was the cruel one by leaving them alone in the shop, waiting to be bought. The gentle energy from my spirit parents' hands began pouring into mine as they stroked them to help comfort me. Intuitively I sensed them tell me to take only one thing from the pouch at this time.

I reached my fingers inside and pulled out a small turquoise stone. This instantly triggered a memory from way back in 1996 when I purchased my very first piece of turquoise. It turned out to be a symbol of my spiritual journey and how it would all unfold through my travels to the Sundance in South Dakota and eventually Arizona.

I remembered the shooting star I saw on the last evening of the Sundance on those sacred grounds of the Lakota people. That was a sign of big changes in my life. It was a deep privilege and honor to be able to walk on their land and witness such a sacred dance. This tree with the Christmas star was here to remind me of the sacredness of that journey which had transformed my life forever.

My spirit father's eyes began looking into mine. They were the same eyes as the raven from the tree, as if he had shapeshifted.

"You have the old turquoise stone to remind you of the deep connection to this land here, the red earth and red rocks that have always nurtured you," he said. "You have gained much strength, much wisdom and some scars too. Now it is time to continue to share with others in all that you do."

"The golden egg, what is the significance of it?" I asked.

"When you have a clear image of your greater purpose here and the illusions are shattered, the egg will be ready to hatch," he replied reassuringly.

My spirit mother then turned to look at me, suddenly transforming into an Arctic fox. She was stunning and so very radiant. Our eyes locked. I reached out my hand to stroke her incredibly soft, deep, thick fur.

The essence of her spirit was entirely peaceful. She was here to remind me of my independence and how far I've come on my individual healing journey. She also wanted to remind me not to take things too seriously and to make more time to be playful.

"That is what got you to the state of exhaustion, you have forgotten how to play." She continued, "Also the purity of spirit. Keep it light, it's so easy to have your spirit tainted by others and your reactions to situations that test your endurance. We can become bitter and angry.

Where have you stored the bitterness in your body? Be aware of this and work with it. Continue to work with your anger. Deep down it is your sadness that needs to be worked with. We all have sorrow, it is a part of life. Those that can work with it, will be blessed to understand the deep teachings from it. We move through our emotional bodies like the river that continues to flow. If we stay in touch with every part of our body, we will remain in that natural flow and life will then become more authentic."

I thanked them both for reconnecting with me in this unexpected way, especially in Sedona. This was the first time they had come through to me while visiting Arizona. As their image faded, I could see a lynx on the trail in the distance leading up to Kachina Woman.

It was time to continue my hike. In some cultures, the lynx symbolizes hidden secrets and psychic powers. I knew there would be a blessing for me as I always receive deeper wisdom whenever I sit with Kachina Woman. It was even more relevant when I then saw a spirit owl in my mind's eye. The spirit of the owl represents great wisdom but also deception, and not always by others but from ourselves too. We can often deceive ourselves and not be conscious of it. When we abandon our dreams in order to please others for example. We can also find ourselves merging with other people's passions and their way of being, while neglecting our own deeper desires. It was time to come back full circle on my own life's journey. I couldn't think of a better or more powerful place to be supported than in the heart of Sedona with all the healing portals.

## The Flute Angel

My friend Layla had connected me with a companion named Jesse, a wonderful flute player who has extensive local knowledge of Sedona. I had arranged for him to take me on some exhilarating hiking trails, some of which even led to sacred caves. I was thinking how wonderful it would've been if he was with me today on this solo hike to Kachina Woman. I was really looking forward to the sacred caves we would be visiting and to the serene sounds of his flute.

I have seen and heard of many miracles and synchronicities that happen in Sedona. Every thought and feeling are magnified. Be aware of what you wish for, as it just might come true!

Within minutes of those thoughts, I heard a flute in the distance. At first, I thought I was imagining it. I continued my hike when I spotted someone sitting on top of the Warrior Rock across from Kachina Woman. It wasn't my imagination, it was real. Someone really was there playing the flute.

"This place truly is a portal of manifestation!" I thought to myself.

Being serenaded on my pilgrimage to the beloved Kachina Woman was such a blessing. I found the perfect spot, put my backpack down and sat with her while being guided into a tranquil meditation to the soothing sounds of the flute. The warmth from the early morning sun felt really good as it beamed down on my skin. I could also sense its rays reenergizing my whole body along with the healing powers of this vortex.

## Kachina Woman ~ Boynton Canyon ~ The Balance Vortex

She stands tall amongst the canyons in the mystical landscape of the red rocks. Not a thing could knock her down. It is said that she guards the Boynton Canyon vortex which is known for bringing balance into your life, and especially for balancing the masculine and feminine energies. Every time I visit here it is such a blessing, but this time I felt even more blessed with the pretty sounds of the flute echoing through the rocks.

The man with the flute had finished playing. He climbed down from Warrior Rock and walked toward Kachina Woman where I was sitting. He immediately handed me a heart-shaped rock.

"You are loved and the Creator is always guiding you on your path," he said warmly.

It was my message from the Universe.

I explained to him how much I had wanted to hear the flute and how amazed I was when I heard his beautiful, melodic music.

"What is your name?" I asked.

"Robert," he replied.

He is middle-aged, medium build with grey hair and a grey moustache. He is known by many local people who live in Sedona and also by tourists who come from all over the world and happen by chance to be blessed by his playing.

You can usually find him serenading the canyon with his tranquil flute in the early morning. Robert is a kind, joyful, enthusiastic soul who spreads his love and light to everyone he meets and wherever he goes. He hands out heart-shaped rocks that he carves personally with an intention of unconditional love.

He was given a message back in 2011 that guided him to play his flute for reiki healing. He says that he plays for the greater good of everything. Robert has committed the rest of his life to playing his flute and spreading reiki healing through the sounds of his music across Sedona and the world. If you run into him on your travels, be sure to give him as much love and light as he will give to you. He continues to make our world a brighter place.

I thanked him sincerely and wished him a blessed day. I continued to sit with the spirit of Kachina Woman. I sat peacefully, soaking in all the beautiful energy that she had to offer. I closed my eyes and I could feel the heat radiating through my body even more.

As I relaxed further, I heard the sweet sound of a

hummingbird close by. They always amaze me with their lightning fast, magical wings. They truly are one of nature's gifts. The hummingbird represents love and joy. My heart was filled with so much joy I felt like it would explode.

I was so grateful for such a blessed day. I always find this vortex filled with many adventures. It seems to be a meeting place for unexpected conversations with kindred spirits. Magical things happen here. I always feel like I'm on top of the world. Make sure to bring a camera with you as the views are simply spectacular.

## White Spirit Horse

Before hiking back, I wanted to go and sit with Warrior Rock on the opposite side. As I was walking across, I remembered the image of the white spirit horse I first saw at Tonto Monument. The image was becoming clearer. I stood by the juniper tree that sits in the center of both Kachina Woman and Warrior Rock.

I sensed that she was thirsty, and visualized myself giving her some water to drink. I was then guided to groom her before climbing on her back. We went for a wonderful trot through Boynton Canyon. She was so divine and graceful.

I was wearing a cream-colored gown which made me feel light and free. I was in a state of such grace and my whole body felt back in total balance. The words 'creating your own destiny on your terms' came to mind. What I truly desired for my life now felt effortless.

It was a clear message for all of us; we are in control of our own destinies. If we can become more in tune with our true nature, we can then manifest our desires.

Pause for a moment and move into your creative imagination. Visualize a white horse, what does it ask of you? What do you seek at this very moment? When you tap into the art of imagination, you will see the images and sense the feelings that will help you understand what is happening in your life.

To access your creative visualization more deeply is to gain a stronger intuition for your life's journey. My wild imagination has brought so many gifts in my own life and to that of my clients and students. I am truly grateful.

## Warrior Rock

The balancer of the masculine, while honoring the feminine, as both energies merge into a spiraling, dancing vortex of bliss and oneness. He watches over her and the valley of the red rocks. I climbed up to Warrior Rock and leaned my back against him to rest, while capturing more of the breathtaking scenery. I felt calm in the stillness of this powerful place. The gentle breeze cooled my body from the scorching sun. As I looked down at the valley below, I could see more adventurous souls making their way up to this vortex.

As I rummaged in my backpack for my water bottle, I noticed something shiny, reflecting the sun's rays back at me. I reached out to collect what was in fact a clear quartz crystal.

## The Secret Crystal

Some kind soul had deposited it here, hiding in the crack of the canyon wall. I held it in my hand and felt a warm energy coming from it. I should imagine it had been left behind as an offering or as a gift for some lucky person to find.

Imagine you are holding the crystal with me. What immediately comes to mind? You can feel the energy of the clear quartz. Your crystalline body and intuition will automatically connect to its vibration. What question do you have for your life right now?

Pause to think about an area of your existence that needs guidance. Now visualize the spirit of the crystal. Alternatively, you may want to hold one of your own crystals. As you focus on the question, hold the crystal in your mind's eye or in your hand.

Tap into the energy and still your thoughts by focusing on your breathing. What is the first thing you see, sense, hear or feel? This will be connected to the guidance you receive. Trust your intuition and your creative imagination, the answers are always deep within you. Thank the spirit of the crystal for its wisdom.

Crystals are magical and great healing stones. There may be a secret crystal hiding and waiting to befriend you somewhere in nature. If not, you can always pick one up at your local metaphysical store. The crystal will choose you just as much as you will choose it. Remember to have fun.

## The Dancing Bells

I put the crystal back exactly where I had found it. Perhaps the next person to find it will also be guided on an adventure. I know the spirit of the crystal was happy that I had connected with it, and it had certainly made me happy.

I could feel the strength of Warrior Rock. I felt glued to it and could have stayed here for hours. I especially loved looking over at Kachina Woman from where I was sitting. I was in an absolute state of serenity.

I slipped into a gentle meditation where I could hear bells ringing in front of me. It sounded like wind chimes. I could feel my solar plexus chakra expanding, and saw a bright yellow light passing through my whole body.

I then saw myself entering a temple where hundreds of bells were ringing. Some were quite small and some were larger. Some were gentle, and others quite loud. They were waking me up, awakening my vibration to a new frequency. They were bringing me to a heightened state of awareness.

I could feel all of my cells vibrating into a new energy. In my third eye, I saw a vibrant blue light. It represented peace, love and joy for all the world. I imagined I was holding a ball of blue light that was in perfect balance and harmony with the universe. I found myself back at Warrior Rock, and threw the ball of light out into Boynton Canyon as an offering to the rest of the world.

May we all live a life of love, peace and endless joy. Take a moment to tap into your own vibration. What does it feel like? If you could change anything about it, what would it be? I have various bells in my healing room. I use them for meditation, and when I am teaching or working with clients. I also like to cleanse my chakras with my bell. If you don't have one, you may now be inspired to get one. It could assist you to fine-tune your chakras and shift your frequency whenever you feel called.

I thanked the spirits of this mystical place, Kachina Woman and Warrior Rock, for such a magical day. I had spent over four hours at this vortex. I was hungry and looking forward to having a nice meal and a soothing hot bath.

## Nine Angels

That evening, after a rejuvenating lavender salt bath, I started to write in my journal. I had been soaking up so much of the intense energy of Sedona and the vortexes that I was in a heightened state of awareness. During my writing I had an image of nine light beings. They were tall, maybe around seven feet or so, and the most peaceful energy surrounded me. Each being was both male and female. Gender did not have any relevance, they were whole.

I have connected with these light beings before, many years ago. I call them angels or beings of divine light. There was one single word connected to each of them. They told me these words were crucial in finding balance on this earth as a human.

One at a time, each angel being came through in my writing with their one word and their message. As each of them stepped forward from the sacred circle that surrounded me, an individual color merged into their pristine bright white aura.

## Peace

The angel of peace stepped forward in a white aura blended with golden light beams. I could see the white and golden rays swirling through all of the cells of their body.

This was their message for the world, "Peace can be found within. Once that is mastered, then everything else will be in the vibration of peace."

## Love

The angel of love came forward in a soft pastel pink aura blended with white. There was a subtle softness to this energy, that of a delicate flower.

They repeated the word "love" three times with this message, "Love thyself, everything changes when you love yourself first."

There was an overwhelming sense of stillness and purity to their aura which tickled my heart and solar plexus.

## Forgiveness

The angel of forgiveness stepped forward with indigo blue blended with the white. This energy was so powerful, and the merging of the two colors was blinding. It took me a while to settle into this vibration. A balance between the male and female energies was very present.

The angel spoke these words, "This is so very difficult for many. How different the outcomes would be if everyone allowed themselves the gift of forgiveness."

I watched as the vibration of the colors danced gracefully.

## Compassion

The angel of compassion stepped out of the circle in a mixture of white light and emerald green. The colors swirled over their heart chakra, then into their upper and lower back before moving throughout their entire body. I noticed an emerald green aura vibrating particularly in the vicinity of their liver.

This angel had such a strong yin and yang energy of divine balance and spoke of how the liver is cleansed when we practice compassion.

They had this message for humanity, "Compassion is the ultimate cleanser."

## Kindness

The angel of kindness came forward with such a gentle aura of white and pale peach. The colors danced around the image of their body. The colors appeared to be alternating. At times I could see only white light and at others only pale peach would be radiating through this angelic body. This angel specifically showed me their breath and the importance of inhaling and exhaling kindness. Allowing yourself to not only receive kindness, but to also be willing to share it.

They spoke these words of wisdom, "Kindness raises the vibration of the world."

## Truth

The angel of truth stepped out with their fierce balance of female and male energy. The colors white and cranberry red blended into a spiraling energy that moved through the center of their body. All of their cells moved into this vortex of energy.

The angel gave this message, "Be who you came here to be, without wearing any masks. Honor your divinity and be true to yourself."

## Wisdom

The angel of wisdom came forward in its androgynous vibration. White and lilac light swirled through their body. The energy was extremely potent and moving rapidly through every fiber of their being. My whole body and every cell was responding to this energy. It was magnificent and seemed so natural.

This angel just kept repeating the word "Eternity". They

were all knowing and a pure reflection of the Universe.

## Faith

The angel of faith came toward me in a pure energy of both male and female. The colors white and magenta moved through their aura from the top all the way down to the bottom. They were blending up and down their body, bringing a motion of balance.

The angel spoke these words, "Believe anything is possible at any given moment in time. Have trust and confidence."

## Joy

The angel of joy was the last to step forward in a bright white energy that was soon taken over by a radiant yellow. It was almost blinding. I felt like a child and wanted to giggle. My body was being tickled all over. I could see images of myself laughing hysterically over the years. This was a feeling of pure bliss.

The angel gave these words of advice, "Every human has access to joy at any given time."

The circle was now complete. I finished writing in my journal and got into bed. As all the light beings faded into the ethers, I felt as if streamers of light were beaming through my body, tucking me in with a blanket of tranquility.

## Chapter Eight

# Bell Rock ~ The Strengthener Vortex

This is one of my best-loved vortexes. I always feel like the energy is tickling me when I am here. This is the one vortex that truly invigorates me. It is also where you can see many orbs and where the presence of Archangel Michael can strongly be felt.

The power here is potent, and many people feel like they are being energized as soon as they arrive in the parking lot. I usually feel slightly disoriented when I first arrive, but this vortex has always helped me to realign and strengthen the balance within my energy centers.

Bell Rock is known as the activator. It strengthens all three parts of the psyche, the masculine side, the feminine side and the balance. Some people describe the feeling here as high vibrational, electric energy going through their entire body. This is the perfect place to bring out your inner child and invite them to play.

I have heard of spontaneous healing happening at Bell Rock. I often connect to the energy of Archangel Michael, and some of my photographs will show blue and purple orbs. You will likely feel the potency of this place around the countless juniper trees that are scattered everywhere. Their twisted branches have absorbed the intensely high energy of the site. Be sure to find a spot close to one of them for meditation and be aware of what you can feel. A sunrise or sunset hike is even more empowering should you choose.

For this hike I chose to go alone. It felt good to be in my own space, to gather my thoughts and to be in silence with the spirit of Bell Rock.

## The Dead Zone

On my hike up, I walked through some gorgeous juniper trees. I was so drawn to them that although I have been here many times before, I somehow ended up going the wrong way. My husband Andy often jokes with me that I have a terrible sense of direction, as I often seem to get myself lost or disorientated in the wild. I found myself at a dead end, so I called it the dead zone.

I called it this because as we go through our life's journey, we reach a time of completion. When we are in that time of reflection, we might notice that what once worked for us, no longer does. Our vibration has changed, we have outgrown something and have started to move into a fresh period of growth.

When you find yourself in the dead zone, go inward. Move into your heart and check in to see what your soul has to say, what your body is trying to tell you. The body knows all your secrets and holds such deep wisdom. Remember to always have a crystal-clear intention for your new journey.

Ask the Universe to support this path and guide the way for you. There will always be signs and nudges from your allies in the spirit world. You will also find yourself meeting all the right people and being at the right place in the most divine timing. Remember that your intention holds the key.

## Divine Destiny

The juniper trees were lending their support as I made my way up to Bell Rock. I now found myself on the right path. The rocks underneath my feet were also helping me every step of the way. The words 'breathe and connect' kept going through my mind. I would use these words as a mantra to guide my way up to the peak as that was my intention.

I have never made it up to the very top, even though I've been here so many times. I began to feel some fear creeping in about making it to the summit. There are only a certain number of ways to make it up safely and it can be a perilous climb if you take the wrong path.

I reminded myself to stop playing small and to step out of my comfort zone. I stopped taking some risks after becoming a parent as it was not just my life anymore, but since realized I had allowed too much fear to enter.

I continued to make my way up, pausing to catch my breath when I needed to. I was getting closer but still had a way to go. It was like going through various levels of energy. Every level had a new vibration.

As I worked my way up I noticed there was a beautiful family in front of me, a mother, father and son, making their way down from the top of the rock. Their energy was like a magnet, I felt intrigued and was strangely drawn to them. They all smiled at me and so I thought I would approach them to say hello.

This wonderful family was visiting from India. They greeted me and stopped to find a perfect place to do some yoga. I found this interesting as I had just been gifted a yoga book from a man that was in the parking lot selling hats. After purchasing my hat, he gave me the book and said it was a gift. It was still in the backpack I was carrying.

Everything is connected, and when you enter a portal, you are already in 'the zone'. The power of the vortexes in Sedona magnetizes everything. You enter a place where everything flows effortlessly and in a synchronistic way. Just another sign that we are all connected in this Universe.

I told them how I couldn't wait to go to India. People carry messages for us, little pieces of our life's puzzle. Pay attention, there are always clues. Everything that you are seeking is also seeking you. It is so important that you allow the magic to happen and don't block it with too much analytical thinking. Sometimes that can mean getting out of your own way.

I continued along the path toward the summit. It started to

cloud over a little, but it felt good to have a break from the hot sun. I rested on one of the rocks for about ten minutes to admire the view, thinking how lovely it was to see a family hiking together in Sedona and practicing yoga.

It was wonderful to witness such beauty, although I was reminded of how different my own life was. I felt blessed to have been raised by an incredibly strong single mother of five, but also sadness for not growing up with a father.

I have always wondered what it would have been like to have had a relationship with my father. I could feel a tugging at my solar plexus and intuitively knew that despite all the hard work I've done to heal that loneliness and my feelings of abandonment, there was still some residual sadness. The body always knows just how much healing can be handled at any given time.

My journey has been one of constant healing, no matter how many years have passed. The dynamics of growing up without a father have affected me in many ways, especially through his tragic story that I have carried throughout my whole life. As we grow, there are always layers wanting to unfold and be shed, so we are then ready to move into higher vibrations.

Instead of running away, I have always surrendered to the healing process. You must never put a time limit on your healing. You just need to be gentle with yourself, and when called, seek guidance from others in the field of professional healing. I honestly would never have come this far on my own journey of empowerment without the guidance of my spirit helpers and my regular spiritual practices. I am also so very grateful for all those that have assisted me on my healing journey.

Sedona is a wonderful place to assist in the healing process. It can be very gentle, but at times very fierce, so be aware of the energies that you are attracting. Remember, everything you focus on has a way of magnifying here.

I had come so far already and was feeling courageous to

make the climb to the top. The closer I got, however, I could see that there was going to be a problem for me. I realized I would need some assistance in safely making it up there. I took in a deep breath and prayed to the spirit of Bell Rock, Archangel Michael and all my guides to help me. I once again surrendered and trusted.

I had now reached the point where I would need to hold onto someone's hand or have someone behind me to give me a boost. I stood there and looked around. There were a few people already at the top and a couple of others still making their way. It was midday by this time, the sun had broken free from the clouds and was heating up the canyon. Behind me was a father with his daughter.

"Are you going up?" he asked.

"I'm hoping to," I replied.

"Here, I'll help you," said the man, who introduced himself as Mike. He first helped his daughter, Hope, to climb up another level and then assisted me.

"Thank you," I said. "Would you mind if I join you both to the top? I don't think I can get up there on my own."

"Of course you can join us," he said.

I couldn't believe what I had just manifested. I had prayed for help while thinking of my father and look what showed up for me, a reflection of that very thing. This is how powerfully healing the spirit of Sedona truly is. I was given a gift to witness the love and connection between a father and daughter, something I have never known.

Two more levels of elevation and we are at the summit. Slowly but surely, we had made it. I felt euphoric, accomplished and so very grateful. We witnessed each other and celebrated finally reaching the top of Bell Rock. There wasn't much room at the summit. Mike found a place to sit, while Hope and I squeezed into another spot.

We were both starting to feel a little dizzy and expressed

that our legs were feeling wobbly. Our equilibrium had to be adjusted. We grabbed some snacks from our backpacks, sipped on water and took in the magnificent view.

I focused on my breathing to help bring me back to balance. The three of us sat quietly and I started to meditate. I began swimming in a swirling yellow energy. As I was spiraling upward into a higher vibration, I felt I was becoming at one with Bell Rock, fellow kindred spirits and with the Universe.

I could see all of Sedona as if I was floating above it. I noticed a remarkable tree, the tree of life. I recognized it from a sacred journey I had once before. It is magical. An array of multicolored ornaments hung from every branch of this vibrant tree. It was a symbol of celebration.

We sometimes forget to celebrate, there are so many reasons for us to be joyful. We get so busy with our everyday lives that we don't take the time to rejoice in our achievements, or those of others. We should honor each other more often.

These ornaments were celebrating one another. They were inspiring each and every one with their radiant colors. I could then see the roots of this tree of life. I was spiraling toward the ground with the vortex energy, going further down to the firm and strong roots and then into an orange energy.

The color orange is a symbol of the sacredness of life. It reminds us how sacred we all are and how sacred our lives are. I breathed into the energy as it entered my body and revitalized me. I felt so light entering the orange vibration. I could hear bells ringing, resembling an Indian temple, as a gentle breeze caressed my face and neck.

I was in the temple of Bell Rock, where hundreds of bells were ringing out in celebration. I could truly feel the magic of this place which had a mystical presence. I was breathing in so much gratitude that I started to cry with elation.

There were other people inside the temple, all wearing white in honor of being alive, honoring every beat of the heart. The heartbeat is in synch with the rhythm of the earth. The body is a sacred temple.

I reached up into the tree of life and plucked a pretty ornament from one of the branches. I held it in the palm of my hand, glittering purple and gold like a Christmas decoration. I could feel the colors going through my body taking me to another higher frequency. Lifting all of us to higher vibrations.

Learn to surrender in the moment of fear. You must trust and loosen the grip. Why do we hang on so tightly to our fears?

I heard a voice, the message was so strong, "Let go and stop hanging on so firmly."

Why are we so desperately hanging on to things? What are you hanging on to? We are already supported by the earth which gives us so much. Why do we find it so hard to trust and have faith?

The wind picked up momentarily, blessing the three of us and the other climbers on the rock with a cooling gust of air. This was an acknowledgement of how beautifully supported we are by mother nature, as sacred souls on this journey of truth.

We are here to find and live an authentic life. We must shatter the illusions of the ego and what we perceive things to be. We are here to be our true selves, to love and give back to all humanity, and help one another. Dig deep, to the very core. Breathe in sacredness and you not only bless yourself, but everyone else too. Take in all that is sacred every day and you will see the changes in your life.

Moving further into my creative imagination, I could see pink and purple flowers in a garden of holiness. They represent each one of us, we are all finding our way home to a Universal meadow. I entered a deeper state of love, and felt the wisdom of the flowers as I watched them come alive, dancing with divine grace in their mesmerizing radiance.

We are all graceful beings of light. Even in moments of challenge or despair, remember your grace and divinity.

Remember the dancing flowers that live within you.

The scene then changed back to the red rocks, spiraling vortex energy lighting up the landscape. Sparks of lightning were piercing the earth, reenergizing the rocks and charging the juniper trees with even more electrical power. This was a symbol of breaking through the old beliefs and paradigms. Everything we have been told or have felt about ourselves.

Gentle rain began to fall, cleansing the earth. This was preparing us for our next journey of rebirth and renewal, can you feel it? Feel the rain washing away anything you are ready to let go of.

It was the most amazing blessing to sit with a young girl and her father, a reflection of the gift that was offered. It was a mirror back to me for what I had desired. This was such a privilege to have witnessed, to have shared in their essence. Especially after the journey I had in the turquoise cave, reuniting with the spirit of my father. This whole experience had been such an incredible gift.

I have never known what it's like to have this special bond and relationship to a father, but on this auspicious day I shared in this powerful encounter. Miracles can happen. I have witnessed and experienced so many magical blessings in Sedona. My heart is full of love and appreciation.

I don't think these beautiful souls will ever know how much of a divine gift they gave to me. I gave deep thanks to the spirit of Bell Rock for this life-changing experience. I also thanked mother earth, all the spirits of this land, and all the Native American and Indigenous people not only on this land, but all over the world. What a glorious day it had been.

## Meditation at Bell Rock

Before we go into a meditation, we will move into a time of contemplation for any area in your life where you feel like you have reached a dead end. Check in with yourself, take a breath and go inward to open your heart and soul.

Before you ask your guides and the Universe to create a new road for you, are you aware of what you first need to let go of? There is always a new path available for you, but sometimes you must help pave it. Even when you think you are lost or have come to a dead end, this is really just the beginning.

Remember that people will always turn up to lend you a helping hand, just like the juniper trees along the trail. They were offering me a helping hand with their branches. The stones were also assisting me, giving me that push to reach another level during my climb up to the summit. The family from India gave me inspiration. The father and daughter gave me hope, healing and kindness. The top of Bell Rock helped me get a different perspective on life. Everything we experience is all very relevant.

Do you recognize any areas of your life that require readjusting? Are there any old belief systems or paradigms you need to break through? Be aware of what you might be attracting through your beliefs and make sure they are not blocking the wonderful gifts trying to come through you and to you.

Imagine you are at Bell Rock. Focus on your intention and see yourself being welcomed by the magnetic, vibrant energy. Breathe into the vortex and allow its spirit to bless you. Put your hands on the red earth and give thanks.

What do you see? Are there any junipers visible? If so, go ahead and sit with one of these magical trees. Your experience will be unique to you, so honor all that you are feeling, seeing, sensing and hearing. Give yourself the gift of stillness. You are on a date with your soul. Bask in the vibrant vortex energies and feel the deep connection and power.

Remember whatever you focus on will be magnetized in this energy, so be aware of your thoughts. If healing is offered, be gentle with yourself and make sure you have the support that you need.

Choose something in your life to celebrate today. How will you express your joy? Perhaps with friends, family or with nature. Whatever you decide, make sure that you truly honor yourself and how far you have come on your journey. Take a look in the mirror and witness yourself. Give yourself a smile and express that joy within and without.

## Wild Jaguar

You are elegant in your demureness. You are black velvet with chocolate brown. You stand for strength and power that teaches me so much. Your eyes carry mysteries only you can know, a portal into an ancient way of being. They hypnotize, but I see kindness and love behind the mystical gateway.

You hold the knowledge to hidden secrets. You are endurance and the gatekeeper of the rainforest. Your generosity gifts a glimpse into wisdom beyond anything I have seen. Dream with me again and we shall sit and watch the stars as they explode into the night sky.

## The Cave of Ancient Whispers

The old man waits to take me to the cave of ancient whispers.

"Come follow me into the secret passageway," he beckons.

As I enter the cave, there are clear quartz crystals all around, lining the walls. I run my fingers across them, absorbing their energy while being cautious not to cut my hands on their jagged edges. He is a silhouette, a memory from the timelessness of creation. He is the past, present, future and beyond, all in one. His whisper is haunting, echoing through the soul like a drumbeat. His voice comes alive within me.

The cave is cool, nestled deep inside the red rocks, protected from the heat. This place is an entry point to the mystery, to the secrets of the earth. If these walls could speak, the stories they could tell of ancient times. The unveiling of the earth, coming back to all that ever was. The creation has no time.

I invite you to come with me. Imagine you are joining me as I go inside. Let us enter with intention. Pause for a moment in stillness. Breathe in and think of an objective. First, I will give thanks to the spirits of the cave that guided me here. I then give thanks for always being in the right place at the right time to manifest adventures, miracles, well-being and joy.

My intention is to enter with respect, and to be open to receiving the blessings and messages that are here for me today. Focus on your intention once again, and come join me as I enter the cave.

I step into the mystery and follow the guidance of the old man. There is a light ahead drawing me further inside. My curiosity becomes me, I follow and notice it is sunlight reflecting inwards from the entrance of the cave. I venture deeper into the depths, continuing to run my fingers across the rough edges of the many crystals lining the cave wall. I notice a smoother spot where I can rest my back against so I sit down.

Breathe with me and stay open to receiving any guidance that wants to come through to you at this time. I can hear the breath of the old man and sense his spirit is close by. I am not frightened. Although dim, the reflection of the sunlight is still visible.

The wise man wants to be acknowledged. I thank him and ask why I was guided to enter the cave, while moving into that part of my imagination where my intuition meets me. My body begins to feel aligned with the energy. I trust the guidance, knowing it is safe for me to proceed.

Stay with me if this feels right for you. Move into the deepest part of your imagination and intuition. There is a place of knowing deep within your being. Only you can identify with this knowledge as it is your unique wisdom. Honor it and give thanks for your gifts.

We are all born gifted with intuition, it is a natural part of our being. If you align with his energy, tap into the spirit of this old man with me, he is our friend. I feel that a part of him wants to be honored and remembered. He is a wisdom keeper. I honor him with gratitude.

The old man begins to speak, "The earth is the keeper of this cave but it is my spirit that dwells here. Feel the oneness of all eternity."

There is a sudden tranquility no words could ever define. I sit in my stillness and listen to his wisdom, like whispers in the wind passing through with a story to tell. The wind has a soothing energy and frequency that carries through into the corridors of our hearts. Again, there are no words. I begin to enter a deeper meditative state. I feel secure.

"This passage you just entered holds the memories of your soul," he explains. "Like a myth through time they will come to surface. The exact recollection you are meant to grasp will come to you."

"What do I do with this soul memory now that I see it and recognize it?" I asked.

I can see a clearer image of him as he sprinkles tobacco beneath my feet and on the ground all around me.

"You breathe it into your heart every day like a sacred pulse that beats with the earth to remind you we are all part of this glorious Universe. We are all eternal beings of light like the reflections of the moon and the rays of the sun. You now have access to this wisdom at any given moment. Remember who you are."

He blesses and honors the journey that I will continue with the knowledge that has been awakened by my soul. He blesses and honors you too. I awaken from a dream within a dream.

This knowledge may not be clear to you right away but will become clearer when you are ready. The whispers of the soul will remain in the cave for eternity. You may come back here at any time.

## Spiraling Vortex

A portal of possibilities is within your reach. Can you see it? Can you feel it? Loosen the grip and let go. Toss it into the vortex, where the spiraling energy will absorb it. Are you ready? When the opportunity calls, pay attention. As you release it to step into your new life of rebirth and renewal, what does that look like for you?

Below is a list of affirmations you might want to choose from and use as a daily mantra. I also encourage you to write down your own. You may be surprised with what comes through.

As I loosen my grip, I get closer to becoming liberated.

As I loosen my grip, I get closer to healing.

As I loosen my grip, I get closer to becoming myself.

As I loosen my grip, I get closer to living the life that my heart desires.

As I loosen my grip, I am free to play.

As I loosen my grip, I come back fully to myself.

As I loosen my grip, I give myself permission to rewrite my story.

As I loosen my grip, my creativity expands.

As I loosen my grip, I feel more joy.

As I loosen my grip, I can breathe again.

As I loosen my grip, I am revitalized.

As I loosen my grip, everything falls into place.

When you are ready, let go...

## The Old Woman in the Tree

I sat by a rock near a fierce flowing river. It was carrying everything away, an act of letting go. The old energy was being transformed, regenerated into something new. In order to embrace a rebirth, one must release all that is standing in the way of the renewal process. You must be willing to relinquish the person you thought you were, in order to manifest through your being the person you were born to be.

So, what is standing in the way? It is us, standing in the way of our own new life. It's hard to believe how much baggage we have carried over the years of our life span. Mental, emotional, and psychological weight that eventually becomes a physical load we carry around. Our bodies have a deep and wise memory. As humans we have survived so much.

The river teaches us not only to wash away our inner clutter, but the element of water also shows us how powerful the act of cleansing is and how important it is to keep the energy flowing. When the energy becomes stagnant, our lives don't flow in a natural way. That is when we can go into a deeper contemplation and to check in with our bodies, not only our physical body, but also our emotional body.

I listened to the sounds of the raging rapids to the point where it became hypnotic. From the corner of my eye, I noticed the tree beside me. In my deeper relaxed state, I could now see an old woman within the tree. It was as if the spirit of the tree was coming to life.

"My imagination is on overdrive," I thought to myself.

## My Old Familiar Friend

The old woman transformed into the image of an owl. The spirit of the owl watches over our decisions. Big or small, she sees them all. Right or wrong, she guides the way. I used to be afraid of her, scared of my own power. I ran away for so long, until I could run no longer. I stopped to clean the mirror and get a clearer view of myself. It was then that everything changed. I had attached my old friend to the superstitions of death. But she is death, in a sense, for she is rebirth.

My old familiar friend has always turned up at important times in my life to nudge me into the next chapter. I now embrace her and honor her wisdom. She sits at the peak with the perfect view. Full of power, she flies steady and high right through the night. She is the owl of wisdom, in charge of time.

How will you choose to use your time and live the rest of your life on this earth?

# Part III

# Interweaving

## Chapter Nine

# The Shaman's Cave

It was seven in the morning, and a good day for a hike. I was really looking forward to going to the sacred Shaman's cave. Jesse had told me about this powerful healing place on our brief meeting a few days ago. I was intrigued. It was a long hike to get there, but I was up for the challenge. I was also excited to hear more of Jesse's flute playing.

He is so talented and can take you into a deep place of tranquility with the sounds of nature through his bamboo instrument. I was lucky to see him perform at one of the hotels, so I already knew I was in good company with his kind and patient nature.

Even the starting point for our hike wasn't the easiest place to get to. We had to drive down a dirt road which was very bumpy at times. We eventually managed to find a parking spot fairly close to the trail head access at the hilltop ruin.

Twenty minutes into the hike, I was starting to feel the heat already and we still had a long way to go to get there. I had to be mindful of the prickly cactuses on the trail, and my arms and shoulders felt like they were starting to burn. I could feel my resistance.

"Not another spiritual initiation," I thought to myself. "What have I got myself into this time?"

My ego was taking over with thoughts of regret. My spirit always knows when big shifts are about to happen, and the fears were creeping in which could sabotage my spiritual progression. I started to panic for a brief moment, my mind looking for the closest exit, but there was no exit. I was already on the trail surrounded by the sacred, red earth.

I took a breath of courage and trusted the guidance from my

teachers. I reached into my backpack for my jacket to protect my arms from burning any further, took a sip of water and continued along the trail.

I thought about the unseen spirit world that continues to guide me on these amazing adventures. The great mystery that unveils itself, despite the numerous disappointments, trauma and sadness I have experienced in my physical reality. Spirit has helped me find such independence during many heartbreaking times. That was when the journey of truth began, but it was also a journey of immense power. I have acquired an inner strength from entering my interior world, although with it came responsibility and accountability.

The dark night of the soul is an arduous path, one I have been down many times, perhaps too many. But like a caterpillar going into the cocoon, it was a transition I had to make. I just didn't know how long the metamorphosis into my new life would take. At times it felt like it would never end. I thought about how challenging life as a mother can be, and about my marriage and how my husband and I were beginning to struggle.

The closer we got to the cave, the more I started to question everything. The sharp cactuses along the trail prompted me to think of life's challenges as they hooked and tugged at the bottom of my hiking pants. A reminder also to be mindful of where you tread. The feeling of butterflies in my stomach was getting stronger.

The energy of the cave was starting to push a lot of buttons for me before we had even arrived. I thought of all the training I have done over the years, all the endless work on myself, the travelling, the studying, and expanding my business so I could be in complete service to others, while at the same time, mothering my three, beautiful children and trying to keep my marriage alive. Although demanding a lot of myself, I was certainly fulfilling my purpose on earth, as more students and clients were finding me.

After what seemed like a never-ending trail, one more level of elevation followed by a slight dip and we could finally see the cave. We reached a cliff edge with a large dropdown. I was grateful for the added security from my hiking boots as we walked along this narrow section. The scenery was surreal, a natural gift. This is a very sacred place where lots of people come to pray, meditate, perform sacred ceremonies and find inner serenity. As we approached the cave, Jesse told me that some people even camp here overnight.

"Wow, I bet their dreams must be amazing," I said.

There was a small opening with stairs that would lead us inside. We could feel the presence of immense power before even entering the cave. I breathed with the spirit of the cave and marveled over the sensational view.

It was time to enter the journey. As I stepped through, the first thing I noticed on the wall of the cave was a caterpillar. I felt this was a good sign for what was to come. A symbol of transformation into the next stage of my life. I found a place to sit down and within minutes, as a well of emotion streamed from my eyes, I found myself sitting in a metaphorical puddle of tears. I had entered a healing portal. The Shaman's cave was shielding, and I felt supported by the spirits here. I was feeling so raw and vulnerable as I entered this second stage of my existence, and began embracing life as a mother, wife, teacher and student.

An unexpected grief had come on; I needed to let go of all the heaviness in my heart. There was no escaping it. I sat being very still and very present with the discomfort and the pain.

I started feeling much gratitude for my husband Andy, even though we were having challenges in our relationship. I sent him so much love with pink light as we moved through this whirlwind of chaos. Our marriage was falling apart like a house reduced to rubble by an earthquake, and I didn't know what to do. I prayed with a humble heart to the Creator for guidance, and to help me navigate the storm.

I sent so much love to all those in the world struggling to make their relationships work, endeavoring to find peace through the murky waters. Striving to keep their families together because they know that deep down, love still resides. Perhaps we all just got lost somewhere on the busy highway of life. There are exit signs, but some miss them because they are not paying attention, and others choose to ignore them, continuing to drive down the same old road. Sometimes, you just need to finish what you started as the story is not yet complete. Next I began healing more childhood wounds.

"It's all coming at once in this cave," I thought.

The energy was intense. I was so grateful that Jesse and I were the only people there and for more soothing sounds from his flute. I was holding on tightly, digging my fingers into the floor of the cave, while the energy was coming through like a hailstorm. I continued to watch the caterpillar crawling which gave me hope that at some point my life would transform.

After what has felt like a lifetime on this path to healing, I am continuously renewing. With every healing comes reformation. I prayed that I may continue to be a divine channel of grace for my children, my husband and my students.

All the years of my life started to flash before me, from the very beginning when I took my first breath outside my mother's womb. The pages and stages of my life became very real as I relived the memories to help heal and empower more areas of my mind, body and spirit.

I then made an offering to the Shaman's cave, a sacred stone that represents my truth and my heart. As I looked at this stone, I could see the wise man that reflects through me and the Goddess, the free-spirited woman that resides within. I breathed this in as both aspects of myself merged gracefully together in perfect harmony.

I honor my sacred temple, my body. I'm not afraid to express myself, I can't hide away anymore. My creativity is bursting; the more I heal myself, the more access I have to this unlimited creativity. I'm ready to express my being to the fullest and stay true to my authentic self. The gentle side, yet also fierce side, the fire within that stands up to truth and continues to express every part of me.

As I looked more deeply into this stone of truth I could see veins. The blood that entwines my family and all of my soul pod as we find each other once again to reunite in this lifetime and see the transformation of the world together by bringing it back into balance. Balance is the key to everything.

I looked through the stone again and could see a cobra snake. I was not afraid for it had great wisdom to teach. I saw my wolf pack howling, surrounding me, reminding me of my family. Not just my bloodline, but my soul family too.

I then saw the owl, her spirit as she always comes to me, guiding and protecting. I offered this sacred stone to the spirits of the cave with immense gratitude.

I got up for a moment and went over to an opening in the wall of the cave. It was perfectly circular and large enough for me to sit inside with my back supported. The scenery from here was even more breathtaking.

I began to drum, the beat moving through the earth and into my own heartbeat, moving me into a state of euphoria. I saw myself dancing inside the cave. All of my spirit allies united with me, as we danced together in celebration.

I now invite you to join me. Take a moment to move your body, releasing any tension. Let your body create art through your sacred temple as you continue to dance. Feel the freedom as you imagine you are here with me in the Shaman's cave. Tap into the healing energy it has to offer you. This is a place of empowerment. The Shaman's cave can be a challenging journey for some, but is well worth the effort should you choose to take the trek.

Enter the journey with a clear intention and you will feel the transformation. The fire that was born inside of you, give it permission to burst and explode into a beautiful rainbow of the most vibrant colors as you continue to heal and evolve on your sacred journey of empowerment.

This is the cave of truth, be raw and be real with yourself. This is a portal for knowledge and deeper understanding.

The caterpillar had now gone, I could no longer see it. It was ready to begin its journey of transformation. What is inside of you getting ready to transform?

## The Shaman's Cave Exercise

Visualize that you are standing at the entrance of the cave. Inhale deeply and think of a clear intention before entering. Once you have your goal, say a prayer or a blessing and make your way inside. Be sure to thank the spirits of the land and of the cave. When you are ready, you can begin the journey.

Visualize yourself sitting inside of the cave. Take in another deep breath, releasing any stress and mind chatter. Surrender to this moment and let go of any resistance. Honor whatever feelings may come up for you.

What are you currently seeking in your life? Breathe it in and then let it out, freeing yourself from attachments and outcomes. Be still in the silence of the cave. Imagine you see a caterpillar. Connect to its spirit and be aware of what you are feeling, sensing or seeing. How does the spirit of the caterpillar make your feel? What does it remind you of?

Call on your power animals or spirit guides to join you. Ask them for any wisdom they may want to share at this time. You may also have something to ask them. Perhaps to ask for guidance in a particular area of your life. Make sure to write down your experience in a journal so you can reflect back at a later date.

Now reconnect to the spirit of the caterpillar, is it still

there? Has it entered its cocoon, or already transformed into a butterfly? Breathe in the word 'metamorphosis' and imagine it in your mind. Write it down and describe what it means to you. How relevant is it to you at this time in your life? You might like to write a poem or a few lines using this word as your prompt.

Bring your attention back to the Shaman's cave. Allow the spirit of this mystical place to bless you. Trust in the process of your unique path as it unfolds during this time of rebirth and renewal. Breathe in the word 'gratitude' three times. May you continue to have beautiful blessings on your journey.

## Moon Dance

She is grace, she is power, she is divine. My grandmother, my mother, my sister, my friend. She holds all the knowledge of the galaxies but does not reveal everything. She is an enigma, like no other, she will give you clues but will never show the whole truth. It is your part of the journey to unveil the secrets behind her transcendent glow.

She will dance with you and sing with you, and whisper poetry. Listen closely, the deepest mysteries reside with her. Pay attention, as she will move you in ways you could never imagine. She will free your soul.

Her vibrancy lures me in. She is hypnotic and alluring, seducing the creation within me, awakening my sensuality. I am safe to explore the natural rhythms within my bountiful body. It moves to each beat of the drum and to the sound in the wide-open space of the red canyon.

The full moon so close I can touch it. So bright that it radiates through me, reflecting off the canyon walls. She is magical, she is me, she is you.

My feet bare on the red earth, each beat moves through every pillar of my being. It is a gathering of old souls. We dance and dance, hour after hour. I am entranced under the spell of Grandmother Moon. Her grace lit up beneath my feet, her beams illuminating every part of me. There are spirits everywhere, yet it feels like just my moon sister and I, whirling through the galaxy in a universal dance of divine sisterhood.

## Kindred Spirits

We will find one another on the hiking trail of life. With similar pursuits, our hearts merge to form one. Our essence recognizes the other wounded souls trying to find their way back home to belonging. We all yearn to belong. Our eyes see so much and our souls have endless stories to tell. We laugh into our bellies like beating drums as our hearts pound together in joy. We will always find each other even though sometimes it feels like forever...

## Enter the Trance

I am in a trance of oneness. With all of creation I dance, hypnotized by the light and beauty of the world I perceive to be the real essence and existence of earth. Let us stay in this mesmerizing haze for it can move mountains into a forever joy.

I can feel the laughter of the earth, giggling like a child frolicking freely on a summer's day. The warm breeze tickles our cheeks and ruffles our hair. The butterfly has earned its place to roam free, to be the greatest expression in all its glory, leaving a trail of letters that spells 'freedom'.

Allow yourself to express your truest nature. The corridors of time expand, opening windows in every room. The hall of mirrors reflects your authentic self, the identity of your soul. At the end of the passage an ocean awaits, so you may enter the great cleanse and rebirth. Are you ready?

Take a step forward into your newly designed life. It was orchestrated many years before you entered into this earth, in a faraway place only your soul knows. It is time to resume the great renewal, but on your terms. This is your life.

## Moonflowers

They say you are crazy, too raw and emotional, you sense too much, so they say. But did they ever stop to wonder how you are feeling, what you are going through? Did they ever notice your wounded heart?

It is not their journey to judge but to be still in your witnessing. The scars seen and unseen. Who was there to witness your deep despair? Are they the crazy ones, searching in the wildness for liberation, becoming free from the pain they carried most of their lifetime?

Where were you when they were fending for themselves? On your own journey, perhaps fending for yourself? Did you not know that in their darkness, they found a way to blossom? Their souls have been growing. Who says they had to look perfect? Judge not the external.

In their stillness, with a frozen exterior of pain, their interior wilderness is healing. Like a moonflower that blossoms out of the darkness, they have courage to come out at night and become seen as a symbol of strength, not craziness. Pause before you judge.

Moonflowers are a species of night-blooming morning glory. They are magical. Did you know they attract bats and night-feeding moths? I find this fascinating, as they are a great symbol for rebirth and renewal.

Some of us are terrified of bats and scared or irritated by moths. Bats can be frightening, but some find them to be beautiful. I like to watch them fly but wouldn't want one to land on me. I have always felt a deep connection to moths. They remind me of little fairies. I enjoy watching them flutter about. They are a doorway to hidden knowledge, wisdom and manifestation.

## Chapter Ten

# The Birthing Cave

In the womb of the divine Mother, far beyond the night sky, stars fall in curiosity of this place. Behind the years of laughter and forgiveness, she is the wind, the rivers and the great ocean. She is the divine Mother of serendipity, the temptress of lust, igniting the fires of creation into fireworks of celebration for you and me.

We must never forget that the earth belongs to us all. We must nurture her just as she nourishes us. We all come from the womb of eternity.

It was day two of my sacred pilgrimage with Jesse. Today was the day we would visit a powerful and very special place he had told me about.

"You will love this place, Rosanna," he said, in his gentle and calm tone.

I couldn't wait to go as my curiosity was growing and the energy in my belly was getting more intense. Our bodies' wisdom will always tell us when something important is about to happen. Do you ever get that feeling in the pit of your stomach when something is about to shift in your life? You can feel the energy brewing even before it takes place.

We began our hike to the Birthing Cave. It was about two miles there and back and a fairly easy hike except for the steep climb as we got closer. It started to get slippery with a lot of cactuses along the trail, so we had to be extra careful. It was a gorgeous sunny day, in early May and the landscape was exquisite.

As we walked, I began humming a tune. This is something I do when out in nature and extra liberated. I was feeling especially free amongst the trees and the red rocks. We were getting closer, and I was really beginning to notice the power of this spiritual place. The presence of the divine feminine energy was abundantly clear to witness here.

As we arrived, I was in awe and could not believe the resemblance of the sacred, feminine body temple. I looked up and my first thought was how would I possibly get through the small opening into the tiny cave? It certainly wasn't going to be easy!

I felt that inner tug of resistance once again, wanting to run, but knowing I had to surrender. It was all part of the process. I was thinking that climbing up would be a real challenge, but Jesse kindly reassured me that it wasn't as difficult as it looked. He offered a hand to assist me in getting up there.

Jesse has a small frame, but he possesses such strength and balance. I had to walk sideways along the cliff edge, at least that's what my body was telling me to do, instead of taking the more direct route, which was virtually straight upwards. I held on to the sides of the wall with a firm grip and continued to breathe. I was scared, as it was easy to fall if I moved my body in the wrong way.

I was getting closer to the small cavern nestled high up in the rock face. The closer I got, the more I could see the incredible similarity to the female anatomy, and I now understood why it had been named the Birthing Cave.

Within its mystery, you also get a sense of the Virgin Mary, the wise woman and the mother. I took a deep breath and clambered inside. I was finally in the womb of the great, divine mother. It was surreal, I felt so completely blessed to be a woman as I took in the incredible scene before me.

Just as I was experiencing overwhelming euphoria move through me, a new sense, one of claustrophobia, started creeping in. I focused on my breathing so I wouldn't go into a panic. Honoring this sacred journey, I surrendered to it. I closed my eyes and began to find a balance.

The word mother echoed through my being. To be a mom is an incredible honor. I was really embracing and honoring myself in this role as part of my life's journey. I felt so much warmth inside of this sacred womb.

I thought about my own mother and all the struggles and challenges she has had to endure in her life. I sent her deep love and gratitude for bringing me into this world, and for fighting for me when the doctors had told her to abort me. They told her that neither of us would survive if she continued the pregnancy, but she believed in me and my purpose. Her deep love, faith and intuition guided her against the doctors' wishes. This is how us humans should always feel. We need to treat our life as a sacred pilgrimage, no matter what cards we are dealt.

I continued to breathe into this moment of beauty. I felt so much strength and wisdom coming through me, it was beyond words. This was one of the most powerful experiences I ever had as a woman, since giving birth to my three, beautiful children. That was the greatest honor of my life.

I began sending all three of my precious kids so much love from this incredible cave. The deep bond and soul connection as a mom can never be broken. A rush of energy moved through me, an overwhelming love that I could not define. These feelings that were moving through me, I just had no words for. I felt so grounded and incredibly close to our earth mother.

A memory surfaced of when I first camped out at the Grand Canyon. That had been such a powerful experience, I had felt the heartbeat of the earth, like she was merging with my own. That was the beginning of a life-changing experience, but this was a little different; it felt like my soul was getting ready to re-birth my creativity.

When I was growing up, I never really saw myself as a creative person. I had what I would describe as an awkward kind of creativity, deeply rooted within my visions. It was always hard for me to express or put into words the vivid imagination that I was born with. Back then it felt like a curse, but as I grew older and explored my spiritualty, I learned to embrace it.

After being diagnosed with dyslexia and Asperger's syndrome, it finally started to make sense to me. The pieces of the puzzle began to fit together. That was when I fully welcomed being neurodivergent.

Although my imagination was always expanding, it took me a long time to accept it. There is such liberation when you finally know who you are. Getting there, however, is not always easy, but can be very rewarding if you stay the course. We sometimes get diverted off our path, but that's okay, as we need to learn the lessons and embrace the blessings we would otherwise not have encountered.

I was so truly grateful for this moment of serenity. It was rejuvenating each cell in my body as I experienced this sensation of total rebirth. Every fiber of my being was immersed in the stillness of this moment.

Pause for a while, take a deep breath and tap into the energy of the Birthing Cave. Imagine you are here with me. I am sending you so much love and serenity. Can you feel it? Inhale oneness and joy. Take in another breath and then let it out.

I could hear the sweet sounds of Jesse's flute, serenading and enlivening every part of my body. I surrendered to any fear I was present with. Fear of the unknown, fear of this very journey. Now tap into your own fear. What are you afraid of? Stop for a moment to really think about it. Allow yourself to be fully present and honest. Embrace your fears as they are our teachers.

We are all just wandering souls trying to find our way. Reach deep inside of your sacred temple to capture more of the true essence of your being. Let your divinity shine through. Take this time to breathe in your new journey ahead. Welcome it, embrace it.

Prepare, gather and collect all the things that will symbolize this rebirth process for you. It could be a crystal, a flower, or any object that has deep meaning. Think of the color that best represents this ritual of renewal. Breathe it in and feel it expanding throughout your body.

I started to breathe in all the colors of the rainbow. Suddenly, my pulse was racing, my heart was pounding through my chest, and I was becoming frightened. It felt as though the womb of the cave was pulsating, like it was having contractions. With each contraction, I seemed to be gradually pushed further out of the cave. I could feel pressure on my back as I endeavored to keep my balance and not look down or panic.

I immediately called out to Jesse to come closer to the cave entrance, in case I fell. My heart started beating even faster. I tried to get in synch with the spirit of the cave. I managed to catch my breath before I really started to panic.

"Breathe with it," I kept telling myself, "just breathe. Don't fight it, become one with it."

As I expressed my deepest gratitude for this experience, the panic began to subside. I gifted to the spirit of the cave a stone I had found during my hike along the trail.

Jesse reached out his hand to assist me as I emerged from the cave and was 'birthed'. He welcomed me on my new journey of renewal. I felt balanced as feelings of bliss moved through me, and began humming a tune of re-birth. A gift from the divine mother.

I found a spot to lie down while I allowed the new energies to settle within me. The heat from the red rocks felt wonderfully welcoming to my body. I continued my song, expressing myself in this new form without any limitations.

The melodic sound of Jesse's flute echoed through the cave, cleansing the womb in preparation for the next brave soul who would enter. I was beaming with love and gratitude. I thanked Jesse for one of the most glorious days of my life.

Enter the journey of your divinity and embrace all that you are. There is always another opportunity to reenter this world in a new frequency. Every day is a fresh start. Are you ready to come out of the Birthing Cave and into your new world? The wisdom in the stillness is profound. The integration and emergence into oneness as you rise into your new life is so rewarding. We just need to have the courage to get there.

## Mystic Meditation for Rebirth

Visualize that you have travelled here. How do you choose to enter the Birthing Cave? You are now inside this tiny cavern, back in the womb of the great mother. Feel the power of mother earth supporting you. Feel her love. Invite her to support your new journey as you get ready to be birthed.

When you are ready, feel yourself being pushed out of the womb. Who is there to catch you? It could be a spirit guide, power animal, angel or departed loved one. Feel yourself being embraced, welcomed and celebrated. Use your creative imagination. Expand your vision and pay attention to how your body is feeling.

Reach for a piece of paper or your journal and write down the first word that comes to mind. How does this word make you feel? Now visualize a color you connect with at this moment. It could be the same color you tapped into earlier or a new one emerging. How does it make you feel and what does it represent for you? This is your new journey of rebirth. How will you choose to celebrate? Most importantly, this is about honoring yourself and creating a new life that is aligned with your heart's desires. There are so many secrets within you waiting to be unearthed and revealed.

Take a moment to breathe in this new energy. You have waited for this moment for so very long and now you have created it. I celebrate you, I honor you.

## Re-birth Ceremony

What song would represent your new re-birth? Sing this new song to yourself. What objects would you take here with you? Don't forget to also bring deep gratitude for being alive and here on this earth at this very crucial moment in time. You may even wish to bring a flower or bouquet with you. Which flower would symbolize re-birth for you?

## Re-birth Ritual

Once you have captured, honored and acknowledged who you are, your understanding of yourself will become even clearer. There will always be 'stuff' to process, but when we are willing to take a deeper journey, that is when everything changes. You will get to know yourself even better.

Pick a date for honoring a re-birth ritual for your new path. Integrating all that you already are, and welcoming who you are still becoming. You have left parts of yourself behind and are ready to move forward. Your authentic self is wanting to shine through like the first rays of light at sunrise.

The best part is that you get to choose who you want to be for the rest of your life. Invite others to celebrate with you and don't forget about your dear spirit allies. They are always here to assist you. It's all about coming back to yourself and unleashing the free spirit within.

## The Crystal Vortex Cave

The following day Jesse took me to yet another cave. He told me that the energy would be completely different and that it was only a short hike to get there. I was glad to hear this after yesterday's intense experience at the Birthing Cave. Although an incredible, life-changing experience, I was looking forward to a much lighter day today.

Getting to the Crystal Cave is not for the fainthearted. There was one area along the trail where we had to jump over a large gap between the canyon walls. It was pretty dangerous, but thankfully we made it across safely. There was a couple ahead of us, also trying to get to the cave. They decided not to go any further as they felt the jump was too risky. One slip could cost you your life.

The Crystal Cave is another spot in Sedona with wonderful scenic views. As we arrived, such pure, light energy radiated from inside. Jesse and I settled in, finding a comfortable place to sit. I started to drum in honor of the spirits of the cave, and especially the Native American people that came before us. I reminded myself how privileged I was to walk on this land.

While I drummed, Jesse played his flute. The spirits of the cave were very happy and I started to see orbs. I hit the record button on my Dictaphone as I continued to drum, entering a blissful trance state. These are the words that came through:

The reflections of our souls intertwine into a beautifully woven blanket within the mirror of our divinity, our vibrations, the very essence of who we are. We mirror back to one another our radiance, and cross over the bridge to the next journey in the waters of the ocean, the depths of the soul. Reaching under, and digging beneath the crystalline earth where all the secrets are hidden.

Walk firmly, yet gently, and stand tall on your journey. You are always aware and awake, ready for new experiences. New adventures are waiting beyond the horizon. Beyond ego, lies the most precious gem, the mystical you, a reflection of the sea on a glorious day. The waters from forever are the ocean's dreams of eternity.

Honor the sacred masculine and feminine within, while breathing in turquoise, empowering you with each breath. The dance of the crystalline vortex, as swirls of turquoise and quartz crystal move into balance.

There is a new rhythm when you merge, honoring one

another and bringing a powerful equilibrium. The fire within is rising, clearing away any doubt about who you are. You become one, swirling into a gentle lilac color, spreading this love and light throughout the world.

I was entering an even deeper state of serenity. I put down the drum but could still hear the soothing sound of Jesse's bamboo flute. The vibrations of the music echoed through the cave and moved throughout my body. I could see all the cells in my body move into a swirling white and lilac color, rejuvenating every fiber of my being.

I saw an image of Ramana Maharshi. He is one of the sages that I deeply honor. His essence appeared to me inside the cave. In this vision, he picked up a crystal from inside the cave, and then took my hand, transporting me back to his resting place, the sacred Arunachala Mountain.

Ramana brought the crystal to the top of the mountain.

"It's the same, it's all the same," he said. "Continue on your path."

He spoke telepathically as I never saw his lips move. He was known as the silent sage. He gave me his blessings, acknowledging the sacredness of the cave.

I then saw an image of Anandamayi Ma.

"It is the meeting of mystics," she said. "The way you express yourself will change when you return from India. Keep radiating love and joy, especially with your children."

My rational mind took over for a moment, as I thought about how hard it was to stay in this peaceful state when challenged with the daily practicalities of life. We are human beings trying to live a spiritual existence on a day-to-day basis, but situations tend to take over. When we are out of balance, we must work harder to find that equilibrium.

I then saw a glimpse of Sai Baba and Meher Baba, who showed me his mystical eyes. I thought back to when I was first introduced to these sages and mystics. It was at sacred gatherings in England with a Welshman whom they called the wizard.

He would chant the mantras in order to help shift your vibration. It was like praying and speeding up the karma process. These secret gatherings were so very powerful and life changing for me. I am so grateful to him for introducing me to these mystics, as my life has been completely transformed by them.

The wizard had access to a higher knowledge that would make clear sense to me many years later. I still have the recording of our one-on-one session. Every time I listen to it, major shifts happen in my life.

"Go beyond the imagination," Meher Baba explained. "You will come to India to see me when you are ready, but do not rush, your timing will be divine."

In my vision, a cobra snake entered the cave, licking my face. I wasn't afraid, I find cobra snakes to be very beautiful and deeply mystical. I drew in a long breath and exhaled deeply. I grounded myself even more, becoming aware of the coldness of the cave floor while pushing my back further into the rugged wall for support.

I was nicely cooled off by this time from the hot sun that had scorched me on the way here. I was starting to feel even more connected to the spirit of Sedona, and intrigued by the incredible mystery of its existence. I could now see the heart, the center of Sedona as I looked out through a hole in the cave wall.

I had never seen it in this way before even though I had been here so many times. I could see the great-grandmothers and great-grandfathers of Sedona. I knew that more and more people would be called to visit this sacred land.

This truly is a magical place where you enter endless portals of your own essence while being supported by the healing soul of Sedona. Deep shifts, healing and blessings can happen here if you allow it. Talk to the spirit of this mystical place, I can assure you it will listen.

I could now see the silhouettes of two elders, one male and one female.

"There is a giant crystal hidden in Sedona," they tell me. "The frequency is changing again, and more light is coming back here. The root chakra is expanding with more high energy and it will be felt once again. There has been seven to ten years of transition. In December of 2021, more light will start coming back, and new paths will be made for many souls. The place of reconnection can be felt as many kindred spirits reconnect with their soul pods."

As they were explaining this, I had another image. I could see a spiraling vortex of rainbows going through the crystalline energy of the earth. I then began to see the tall light beings once again. I had the first glimpse into their world when they came to me in Canyon de Chelly on a family road trip. They radiate just pure and divine energy.

Next I saw crystalline, citrine energy flowing through the Feminine Vortex and into the waters of Oak Creek. It was radiating in a very high frequency. I could really feel the heart chakra of Sedona expanding, and also the alignment with the throat chakra, helping people to find their voices. The crown chakra was now exploding too, with vibrant rays of purple. The soul of Sedona was evolving.

Suddenly the serene sound of Jesse's flute stopped and there was only silence. I was still as I came out of the trance. My awareness had completely shifted and I could hear a buzzing sound. I looked out of the cave to see two bumblebees playing in each other's energies. I reached into my backpack for my journal and wrote these words.

## Two Bumblebees

Angelic beings of the mystery. Keepers of secrets, keepers of life. In partnership, expanding the Universe with golden energy that radiates through the center of the crystal, taking souls to their truth. See it without the ego present. For a short time, glimpse into their pure splendor and into one spirit. We are here to touch one another with purity and innocence, returning to that place of wholeness. Spreading clear love and joy into the world, they are the wisdom keepers.

## Meditation into the Crystal Vortex

Sit quietly and still your mind. Imagine you are entering the cave. You find a comfortable spot inside, sit down and inhale deeply. Visualize two bumblebees in your mind's eye. You may even be able to hear them gently buzzing. Focus your awareness on the colors yellow and black.

You have made it past the gatekeepers. Show your gratitude to these wisdom keepers. The image fades, you now become conscious of the crystalline energy inside the cave. Allow this energy to bless you as you move into a greater awareness.

Stay open to receiving the blessings that are being offered. Take notice of what you are feeling, seeing, sensing and hearing. Let the crystalline energy fill you with a sense of wonder.

Does anyone meet you inside the cave? If so, who comes to join you? What messages do they have? This is your own unique experience so be sure to honor it. Stay open to new adventures as you shift your perception.

When you have finished the meditation, grab your journal and write down the first thing that comes to mind. It may even be just one word, don't judge what comes through. Be sure to also write down your whole experience so you can refer back to it at another time. Perhaps there will be future messages for you here. Honor the journey and give thanks.

## Emergence into Oneness

I can hear Lia's voice speak deep within me, "We emerge with the earth, the sky, the moon and the stars. We become whatever we inhale, ingest or speak. If we are one with the earth, then we must honor her. As we respect her, we respect ourselves. Merge, child, merge into all that you are. I am a distant whisper in the wind. The echoes of my soul are in all things. We are becoming one, merging into oneness. When we let go of judgement, we release our grip like the autumn leaves, left raw like the branches, naked and vulnerable. That is when you look inside your true self, that is when you rise up into authenticity. It is only then that you will begin the emergence into oneness."

Her words spoke so beautifully through my heart.

# Chapter Eleven

# The Wisdom Lodge

I woke up feeling grateful for another day in Sedona. Jesse had a few hours to spare and offered to take me to another sacred place. He called it the Wisdom Lodge. I was excited for another adventure. Our journey to the lodge was interesting, with cactuses of all shapes and sizes along the trail. It was a lovely, sunny day but not too hot, perfect for hiking.

I was so grateful to Jesse for lending me his drum. I wanted to pack light for this trip, so I had left all of my own drums at home. It was painted black around the edge with pretty colored flowers in the center that brought it to life.

When we arrived, I began drumming outside the lodge to give thanks to the spirits of the land and to ask permission to go in. It is very important to be respectful and to always ask permission before visiting sacred lands, caves and dwellings.

Upon entering the lodge, there was a stillness inside. I could feel the deep wisdom within this dwelling place as if the walls had stories to tell. There was something so profound about how tranquil I felt, as though an aura of serenity was caressing me. It was so soothing.

I opened myself up to receive the healing emerald, sapphire and royal purple energy that was swirling through my body. I found a place to sit down and quietly listened to the wisdom within the walls of the lodge.

I have always had a fascination with holy places, where people come to remove their masks and their armor, and pour their hearts out through prayer. These are places where souls sit quietly for introspection, solitude or to release their emotions.

It is imperative that you feel safe enough to fully surrender and let go. It is also important to honor the presence of the ancient ones, the wisdom keepers that came here before us. This was especially noticeable here, they had left behind such a strong, loving aura that you could feel it immediately upon entering the space.

There was a real sense of belonging. We all want to belong to someone or something. With each breath you belong, you are breathing with your ancestors, with the earth and with all of humanity. We all belong to one another, sharing the same air. If only we could see this, there would be more peace in our society.

I could hear the pretty birds singing joyfully outside. The sweet sounds of love and harmony. Nature is so free and abundant, and generosity is within all of us. We all long to be free from whatever weighs us down in our ever-changing world, and yet we cling on so tightly. To let go is to become liberated.

As he entered the lodge, Jesse started playing a soul-stirring tune on his bamboo flute. I thought about romance and how we all just want to love someone and to be loved by them. It's not always that simple but it should be. I pondered my own marriage and the love that my husband and I have for one another, and how that too was evolving.

We are constantly expanding. Love may come as a storm, or a wave, or as a gentle raindrop in the sea of change. The waves capture one another, merging together into an ocean of love and oneness, reminding us as kindred spirits that each one of us carries serenity within.

Delve into the stillness of your own ocean of love. Stay with it for a moment. If you could love yourself unconditionally, what would that look like?

The haunting beauty of Jesse's flute was moving my consciousness as I now dived into a deeper meditative state. To my pleasure and surprise, Lia and Amber Woman entered the lodge. They are both from different continents but their souls are intertwined, woven together with unfathomable knowledge.

A beautiful spirit basket appeared in front of me on the lodge floor. My precious Inuit guides had also come to join me. I knew this meeting must be of crucial importance for all of these guides to come together at once. My heart was beaming with joy.

They came to show me a calmer journey ahead as I was now closer to becoming my true self. You see, when you are nearing your authentic self, no matter how many bumps there are in the road, it will appear smoother to you.

I could see the hands of my dear spirit allies, all weaving together a blue and purple blanket for me. Not only had they gifted me a basket, but now a beautiful blanket too. I felt like it was my birthday. I was learning how to receive. I was deeply moved but still somewhat curious as to what was happening.

My spirit father was on my left side and my spirit mother sat on my right. All together, they wrapped the blanket around my shoulders. My aura began swimming in an ocean of blue and purple. This was extremely empowering. I felt my body temple becoming stronger on so many levels.

The blanket represented the gentle energy that we all carry within us. It's not all about having fierce power, as the flame can always be dimmed. As I was thinking this, a gentle spirit fire began burning in the center of the lodge.

The ground was then covered with delicate flowers. It had become a sacred garden with the most striking, vibrant blooms. Pretty shades of orange, red, purple and blue filled the inside of this sacred dwelling. I saw red tulips, orange roses and sweet scented lavender divinely decorating the space.

The next thing I noticed was a white tiger entering. The last time I had seen this particular spirit animal was on a New Year's morning, many years prior. He had appeared at my bedside to greet me and wish me a happy, healthy, prosperous and bright year ahead. I wondered what had happened to him. Perhaps I was now ready for his teachings.

He had come to teach me of courage, strength and virtue. The gentle spirit of a white deer also entered the lodge, reminding me of the white deerskin dance my friend Bruce and I had been so blessed to attend on the Hoopa Valley Reservation. It warmed my heart to be reminded of such a sacred ceremony.

My spirit mother guide turned to look at me. Her eyes carry many secrets, and she always has a way of looking straight into my soul. She has seen so much and knows the mysteries of the spirit world.

"Teach your children well," she tells me.

I listened carefully to her words. The white fur around her shoulders highlighted even more of her beauty. My heart burst wide open and tears welled in my eyes before trickling down my cheeks in a never-ending flow of emotion. I may have done some things differently, but I have always tried my very best to be a good mother.

Our world has become so different from how it used to be. Many of us are finding it a challenge to achieve balance. Every pebble that drops into the river is carried to a greater ocean in its unique dance.

I started to drum once more, expressing my gratitude for this blessed day. I was drawn to something resembling a window. We are always given an opportunity at some level to learn the lessons, embrace the blessings, and to grow. It's a calling of the restless soul within, a gentle awakening, a nudge that tells you to pay attention so you can be ready when a chance moment presents itself. When the wind calls, be open to receiving its wisdom, as a clue for the next journey is ahead of you. Most importantly just be yourself and ensure you are prepared for the miracles of wonder.

I continued drumming and started singing a song of gratitude for the spirits of the Wisdom Lodge. I felt so liberated as I melded with the beauty of the scene. In my mind's eye, I could see a gathering of men and women sitting in a sacred circle, praying and chanting. Their forms merged into one and then quickly vanished into the fire. I heard an elder's voice begin to whisper.

"It's the fire of truth," the wise woman said. "Listen to your authenticity and don't let others steer you the wrong way. Only you know your rightful path, it is the journey of the heart."

I looked toward the entrance as seven wolves entered the Wisdom Lodge. Three of them were white and the other four were grey. Their magnificence took my breath away. We played and danced together as we watched the setting sun. A spectacle of bright orange and golden yellow streaked between the fluffy pink clouds, followed by a fiery red that would set the scene before the night sky was finally graced by the silvery light of the moon and stars.

As I watched the fire burning, I saw an image of a tall Native American man, near the entrance to the lodge, that resembled Damon. The color turquoise surrounded him.

"It's been so long, why has his spirit appeared?" I thought to myself.

It had taken me such a long time to heal from the pain I had gone through in the early years of being a single mother with my eldest son.

As I continued to watch the flames in the fire, I thought of the journey of twin flames. I was told a long time ago by a wise woman that they come together for an important purpose, to bring lessons and blessings to one another and to create something beautiful. Most of the time it is not possible to stay together.

After years of sadness, I had finally found peace. I understood that our journeys were vastly different. I was so very grateful for the life I was living with my husband and our three beautiful children. It's a liberating feeling to finally reach that place of acceptance.

It was a brief and peaceful encounter. I thanked and

blessed his spirit for visiting me, my heart beaming with love and gratitude. I also thanked Jesse for bringing me to this deeply, powerful lodge. It truly is a Wisdom Lodge, a place of empowerment, deep healing and liberation. I will never forget what I experienced here and how incredibly connected I felt to the earth and to all beings. This is what it feels like to be in the vibration of pure oneness.

Many people find it difficult to come into the fullness of who they are in fear of being judged. I know I did for many years. If you truly want to live in alignment with your authenticity, then you must not worry about what other people may think of you. The only thing that matters is what you think of yourself. There is true freedom to be found in honoring that.

I felt so refreshed and revitalized after my encounter in the Wisdom Lodge. It was as if we had been in there for months. I was in a complete state of gratitude and my aura was glowing in all my favorite colors.

The hike back was peaceful. Every step was a prayer as I blessed all of those dear to my heart, starting with my family, my friends, my students and my clients. I blessed everyone in my life as I radiated in bliss.

Pause for a moment and think of someone you would like to bless in this very moment.

Now enter the journey. Imagine that you are approaching the Wisdom Lodge. Prepare your intention, and when you are ready, proceed inside the lodge.

What does it look like for you? Is there a fire already burning? Are there any spirit animals or guides waiting for you? Sit quietly and write down your experience. Try not to judge what comes through, and allow the inspiration and deep wisdom to flow naturally.

Be sure to have your journal or a piece of paper handy. You may also want to have some colored pencils or crayons available for this exercise. Create your own Wisdom Lodge, then keep your image close by and see what wonders manifest through you.

## The Twelve Dolphins

They take me to a temple surrounded by citrine crystals with black tourmaline beyond. Twelve dolphins greet me at the gateway. As they frolic around me, the temple gates open and I swim through into a deep ocean of green and blue.

While the sun radiates through the water, six dolphins pass me playfully on either side. Come join in and feel the liberation. Shake off the stress within your body and imagine you are swimming with us. The water absorbs any remaining tension. Let go of all mind chatter or expectations.

This gorgeous turquoise ocean completely rejuvenates you. Imagine the sounds of the dolphins as they invite you on a deeper journey. Now visualize all the vibrant colors are expanding through every cell of your body, as you continue to swim in an ocean of bliss. You feel completely liberated.

## Back to Innocence

White and blue hues merge in the sky among fluffy clouds. An angel with wings high above her shoulders stands in the center of a rainbow. I sit on a cloud with a perfect view of all the pretty colors. It is so soft here.

A rain shower falls from the sky. I dance naked and free with no limitations. I catch the rainbow's colors as they move through me, grasping on to every one. They have formed a ladder. I climb back down from whence I came, forever dreaming with the clouds.

## Lemurian Golden Temple

After many days of hiking in Sedona, I was having fun new adventures through all of the metaphysical stores. I popped into the Atlantis shop, thinking I was only going to be five minutes or so. What I didn't realize was that I was about to enter another time period.

I am a strong believer in past lives and have always found great benefit in going on these deeper past life journeys, not only for myself, but for my clients and students too. I wrote about some of my personal experiences in my first book *Awakening the Divine Soul: Finding Your Life Purpose*.

As I walked inside, I noticed a pyramid-shaped frame with a cushion mounted in it to sit on. The friendly storekeeper greeted me.

"Feel free to enter the pyramid if you like," she said kindly.

This seemed intriguing, so I climbed into it and sat down. The first thing I could feel was my whole body tingling. This sensation continued for about ten minutes. The mind chatter started to quiet down, and I was feeling calm and completely relaxed. I started to focus on my breathing and went into a deep meditation.

I moved through a bright, white light that took me to a Golden Temple. I intuitively knew I was revisiting my past life in Lemuria. I had seen this temple many times on various meditations and journeys. There were citrine crystals everywhere. I saw myself in the scene looking very tall and confident.

As I entered the temple, a tiger came to greet me. She was stunningly beautiful. Her stripes were the most vibrant orange and black I had ever seen, and her face was so striking that my eyes were captivated by her radiance.

She took me to an altar where I saw myself sitting in front of a giant, clear quartz crystal. I was wearing a white and golden gown and I was teaching more than seventy students how to activate their wealth. We were surrounded by eighty-eight citrine crystals. That number stood out very clearly. I had peacock feathers behind my head and around my shoulders. There was a smoky quartz crystal gem on my third eye over my birth mole.

Suddenly with both hands I began turning the large quartz crystal in the center of the room. As it was rotating, it activated all of the citrine crystals and powerful energy started to flow out of them, blessing us with an aura of abundance.

We all started celebrating by dancing and singing. Some of my students were playing harps. Baskets filled with luscious fruits including grapes, figs and pomegranates appeared in front of us. I noticed a gold cobra snake bracelet around my upper arm. Everyone was dressed in vibrant colors and elegant attire.

I was talking to some of the people, and it looked like I was making decisions about sacred geometry and the energies in different places of the world. A yellow-and-black-spotted jaguar sat beside me on my right, he was one of my spirit animals. On my left was a loyal lion. A hawk flew circles in front of me, while a white owl sat on my left shoulder.

My meditation started to fade as I heard someone walk into the store. A woman began talking in a soft tone. She was saying how it was time for people to move into a new energy of abundance and how we are all ready to have a wealth consciousness.

Abundance comes in many forms. I slipped back into my meditation, and caught a glimpse of a glass cabinet. It was locked, but my loyal lion handed me the key. Inside were all the completed works I am meant to write. Some of them I have barely started, others are half written manuscripts, and some are just poetry and song lyrics. I now felt hopeful they would all eventually manifest into actual books.

When I came out of the pyramid, I gazed at myself in the mirror and looked so much more refreshed. The woman in the store was amazed at how much lighter my energy was. I felt thoroughly revitalized. I thanked her for the unexpected healing experience.

Many people come to Sedona for spiritual healing, adventure and to find a deeper connection with themselves. I have been called to Sedona so many times over the past twenty-six years, and the more I visit, the clearer I hear her summoning me back when it's time to return. I continue to reflect on our wonderful family road trips where we visited Sedona on numerous occasions. Our children will remember and cherish those memories for life as will my husband and I.

We are not the only ones that receive healing when we visit sacred sites. It is also an opportunity to give love and respect back to the land and to our dear mother earth. It is important that we honor the spirits too. Everything has a spirit and is very much alive.

When you are connected with nature, you will move into synchronicity where everything will mystically align, as you enter the zone. Stay in the flow of your natural rhythm and you will meet all the right people in the most perfect and divine timing. Also be aware of how intense the energy can get. It's important to stay grounded to balance your mind, body and spirit.

When coming to Sedona, I recommend first visiting the information center. It is also a good idea to hire a guide before going out on some of the more difficult hikes. Always listen to the wisdom of your own guidance.

# Chapter Twelve

# Chakra Merge in the Labyrinth

Whenever I have the opportunity to walk a labyrinth, I will always take it as I find the experience to be so wonderful. It is calming to enter a walking meditation, a divine date with your soul and the land. Before I enter, I focus on gratitude.

It was late afternoon and I decided to head out to one of the several labyrinths dotted around Sedona. On arriving, the energy felt a little different. As I walked between the stones, I went through my chakras, starting from the base chakra and moving all the way through each one.

With the first few steps I saw shades of red getting darker until they reached a rich candy apple. This made me feel grounded as to where I was in my life at that time. As I continued, I saw the red turn to orange, moving into my sacral chakra. This was bringing me back to life in the areas of my passion.

With each breath and step, I could see a bright-burning fire along the path I was taking. It felt warm, expansive and expressive in a sensual way, like it was regenerating me.

My inner voice whispered, "It's the sensuality and expression of self. Don't be afraid of your power or bury it away. Let go of limitations and set yourself free."

It was a clear message to not be afraid of my sensual power.

I was now entering my solar plexus chakra, with such a bright yellow light which moved me into a vision of the giant lemon I saw in Positano, Italy. This made me feel happy, my whole body radiating in a yellow glow, bringing a greater sense of self-confidence.

I kept walking with a sense of both peace and empowerment. I was approaching the center of the labyrinth, as I now shifted into my heart chakra with pale green energy circulating around my chest. I noticed some fogginess in that area of my body, so I focused on my breathing with the awareness of my heart.

I saw the word 'forgiveness' written across my chest. As I tuned into the word more deeply, I became aware of who needed to be forgiven. I breathed into the word before offering forgiveness, first to myself, and then the person I needed to forgive. I had already done some work around this, so I was shedding another layer and now ready to forgive more completely. I drew in another breath, moving deeper into the vibration of the word, while the green transformed into a more radiant, emerald shade. I began to feel lighter and more liberated.

It was wonderful to have the warmth and support of the sun with me during this healing walk. As I reached the center of the labyrinth the sun was getting low in the sky. Dusk is such a special time in Sedona. It is so delightful to watch as the sun sets in all its glory over the red rocks. I gave thanks once again for everything in my life and for this beautiful day.

I paused for a moment in the center to watch a butterfly on a nearby flower and a hummingbird darting between the trees that surrounded the labyrinth, feeding on aphids and sweet nectar, before retracing my steps in the opposite direction, back to where I started.

I could now see a stunning turquoise blue moving through my throat chakra. It was pure and clear, which has not always been the case during times in my life when I was afraid to speak up and express my truth. Once I started owning my voice and was no longer afraid to communicate my verity, so many doors opened for me.

It is much better to vocalize your feelings than to hide them away in debilitating fear. This is a wonderful chakra to work on when you need the courage to voice your authenticity. It may not always please others, but those that honor your feelings are the ones that are meant to stay in your life.

As I got closer to the entrance, I began moving up to my brow chakra. I took a deep breath into my third eye and saw deep indigo mixed with shades of purple. When I tune into this chakra, I always clear it first by imagining I am dusting off anything that doesn't belong and then polishing it so I can activate it further. It is the place of wisdom, clarity, insight and intuition. I always feel this chakra being fully charged when I am in Sedona.

I was nearing the end of my journey, when I saw my brow chakra merging into my crown chakra, radiating in pretty violet light, my favorite color. Since I was a little girl, I have adored all shades of purple. They reflect my true self. I felt invigorated with such a deeper sense of tranquility and empowerment.

As I reemerged from the labyrinth, the sun was setting so beautifully in the sky. It was a magical moment. I admired the bright, golden orange and yellow streaks across the baby blue backdrop. I expressed my gratitude and touched the earth, while all the colors of the chakras began merging within me. I stood there and could feel them dancing throughout my whole body. My cells, organs and all the fibers of my being were dancing with the vibrant hues in joy.

## Chakra Merge Exercise

I invite you to imagine you are walking a labyrinth. You may be able to do this physically, if you are lucky enough to have one close by, or you can go on a walking meditation if you like.

What is your intention or prayer before you enter? Focus on the stillness within, every step you take is a prayer. Be aware of the energy centers in your body, and tune into all the chakras. Visualize the beautiful colors as you scan each of them. Ask the wisdom of your body to speak with you, and listen to the guidance from within.

## Don't Deny Your Destiny

During my time in Sedona, I was so blessed to attend a weekend workshop with gong master Don Conreaux. I always seem to find myself in the right place at the right time. A mantra I like to use often is, "May I be in the right place at the right time to attract all that my heart desires."

I saw Don once before, over twenty-five years ago in the UK at the Mind, Body, Spirit Expo, but until now hadn't been able to attend one of his workshops. I planted the seed back then, knowing that when the time was right it would happen. Always believe in divine timing. We humans get easily frustrated, wanting things to happen quickly. However, in the spirit world there is no concept of time, we are souls of timelessness.

Don's workshop was a small, intimate group and I feel so grateful for having spent time with such an incredible gong master. During the weekend, he and his apprentices asked if there was anyone that wanted to volunteer for a gong healing. My intuition told me that this would be a transformational experience, so I raised my hand.

I was chosen, and asked to sit inside the circle while they performed the healing ceremony. Don and two of the practitioners played gongs in front of me, while the others held the space so the rest of the students would also feel the incredible healing energy emanating from the gong vibrations.

Halfway through the ceremony, I started to feel like I was drunk, even though I had eaten a healthy lunch and had only been drinking water. I then entered a deep, altered state, like a shamanic journey but even more intense. I started speaking out loud to the circle as if I was in a trance. I could see many mystics appear in the room, including some of the sages that I connect with on a higher level. It was very moving, they were all wearing white and the room had transformed into pure white energy. I was feeling lightheaded but kept focusing on my breathing, trying to ground myself.

Some would describe my experience as hallucination. I have never tried hallucinogens but I imagine this is what that might feel like. In all the years I've practiced shamanic journeying and meditation, I've never felt this way before. It was beginning to scare me a little; I was spinning and clinging on for dear life.

I was battling with my ego, that part of me that still wanted to be in control.

"What will happen if I let go?" I thought.

With every breath and resonance of the gong, I let go a little more. The energy was so intense that I could feel my whole body vibrating with it. I was moving into such a high frequency that I started to giggle, which soon turned into laughter and then uncontrollable hysterics. I was being bathed in high vibrational gong bliss. I can only describe this as pure joy, such that I have never experienced on this level. It continued for over fifteen minutes, and every time I tried to bring myself back, I would laugh out loud again.

This bliss eventually levelled out. I felt myself becoming more grounded as I focused on my beloved willow tree. I imagined myself putting my hands on her trunk, while my feet were firmly planted into the earth. I then sat with Willow, my spine leaning against her trunk. She always has my back.

I was slowly coming out of my euphoric state and was now fully present in the room. I felt my feet on the floor and saw myself sitting in the chair. Tears started streaming down my cheeks. It was another release. I wasn't surprised as since I was a little girl, I would often laugh and cry at the same time.

Don was now standing behind me with his hands over my back. He told me I was receiving reiki healing and that I had just experienced a kundalini awakening. I wasn't surprised to hear this as I had moved into such a deep place of Universal connection and oneness like I have never known. He looked me straight in the eyes and said, "Don't deny your destiny."

Those words stayed with me for weeks after the workshop,

probably even months. I realized I had been denying my destiny for years without even knowing it. Trying to balance life as a mother, wife, student and teacher was not easy. There were times I just wanted to quit. This path seemed a bit out there and I wanted to live a more 'normal' life. But what exactly is normal anyway?

I later learned the true meaning of those words, to just be myself and keep coming home to me, embracing all that I am. It has taken me many years and I am still trying to master that. Perhaps it is something that comes with age and years of experience.

Are you denying your own destiny? If you knew what that was, what would you do with the knowledge and how would you embrace all that you are?

I was trying to live a spiritual life as a walker between the worlds but still found myself worried about what others might think of me. I was born with a wild imagination and was paving my way through these gifts.

After the powerful experiences I already had in Sedona, visiting the sacred caves and all of the vortexes, this ceremony felt even more heightened and supported. They had prepared me for this moment. I was truly grateful for this life-altering and euphoric healing. If it weren't for all the years of inner, deep healing work I've done on myself, I don't think I would have been ready for it. Once again, I was in the right place at the right time, with the earth's portals and the calling deep within, answered in so many mystical ways.

When our body is in total alignment with the earth's energies, it can be truly profound. I recognized where I was experiencing a lot of fear.

Is fear the driving force in denying *your* destiny? What would your life be like if you arrived at the place of your heart's desire? Are you truly ready for it or are you still buying time? What is the real reason why we deny ourselves from fulfilling our deepest desire? Perhaps we don't know what we will do with it when it arrives and so we sabotage it. What if we just accepted with grace?

When I think of grace, I think of a radiant flower that has blossomed, its delicate petals intact, no matter what winds and storms have moved through. Grace is all the divine power that ever was and ever will be. Grace is presence. To accept these gifts, you must be fully present with yourself, every part of you. You must also know who and what you are in order to fulfil your divine destiny.

Many are just existing without unwrapping their full potential. You must bring yourself back full circle on your journey of oneness. Move through the upheaval, the rage, the grief and the joy, and be fully present with the here and now. Thoroughly feel all of those emotions, witness your wounds, and love yourself even more.

Seek out healing professionals to help you do the inner work. I would never have made it to this place on my own journey without guidance from others in this field. When you are ready, move into a rebirthing, a renewal of your true self. You will be forever grateful.

## Re-Emergence of Self

When we deny our destiny, we stop the flow of life and step out of our natural rhythm. We enter the 'delusion of illusion' with the hows, whys and ifs. This is not part of our original journey.

When you surrender into acceptance and embrace the life that was mapped out before you even entered this world, your perception completely shifts. You keep your natural flow moving, and not only do you feel inspired by your life, but you inspire others too. All the events in your past, all the trials and tribulations have shaped you for this moment. They have led you to this crucial point in time, where you must not deny your destiny. Are you ready to reemerge?

## Antelope Canyon

Creation's mystery, you lure wounded souls unexpectedly to your photogenic wonder. Into the sacred lands of the Navajo. I thank you. You beckoned me inside your portal of the heart, not knowing how closed was my own until I entered yours. There you lifted the veil for me into a deep splendor. Your sandstone walls with their ever-changing hues of red, orange and yellow captured a part of my spirit. Your extraordinary grace and magical, transcendent existence is awe-inspiring beyond imagination. I feel invigorated and renewed.

## Re-Activation of Fate and Timelines

You will reach a certain point in your life when the dream you left behind becomes reactivated. It doesn't matter how many years have gone by, it was necessary to endure that test of time in order to reactivate your fate and timelines. When you are aligned with the Universe, and you are both ready, the part of your destiny that was activated during a different time in your life will reemerge once again, bringing you to the place where you left off. You probably thought it was gone, but it never was.

If you keep your dreams alive and your heart open to love, they will someday realign, and you will understand that it was all part of your unique journey. Thank the creator once again for all the gifts you have been given. Can you remember a dream that you left behind? Pause for a moment to reconnect with it. Are you ready to reactive this dream? How will you choose to honor it?

## The Butterfly Emerges

She sings in the dark, waiting to see her own light. As she tunes her voice, a flicker enters the darkness. Her call pierces through the night, engaging the luminescence of fireflies that dance through the vastness of nothingness.

She has waited her whole life to capture this glimmer, this

spark of life. She embraces her emptiness as she fills her breath with laughter, cracking throughout the cocoon. The butterfly sings her own unique song. Bewilderment leaves, she is free from the darkness.

# Part IV

# Imagination

# Chapter Thirteen

# Twelve Orcas

I was back home on Vancouver Island. I knew my mind, body and spirit would take a while to readjust from the transformational journey in Sedona. The rest of me would need to catch up to the vibrational body I was shifting into.

Andy and I were long overdue for a date night, so we booked a weekend away in Victoria. I was reminded how crucial it was for us to have date nights, a romantic time away from all the running around and chores. This is one of the keys to keeping a marriage alive.

We had a lovely evening together with dinner and wine, and then later I slipped into the dreamtime. I had a powerful dream that I didn't want to wake up from. One of those big dreams where you feel like you are still in the scene upon waking.

I was swimming in the ocean when twelve orca whales began circling me. As I watched them, they then formed a line. As I started swimming closer to them I saw my younger son in the water. I was experiencing some anxiety, as I thought he may be drowning. My motherly instincts took over and I wanted to rescue him.

I was having a hard time keeping my head above the surface when one of the whales swam underneath me, lifting me out of the water. When I looked over at where my son was, he was swimming freely and confidently. His energy was so joyful, having all the whales supporting him.

This dream felt significant. It was all about family and my ancestors. I got clear messages for all three of my children and was no longer worried about my younger son. The spirit of the orcas showed me the strength and power of their medicine. I felt a profound and deeper connection to my ancestors and knew they had my back. We are all part of the great mother. She nurtures us in the womb of an endless sea. The spirit of the whale protects us with incredible strength. It represents creation, healing, family and balance.

The next day, Andy and I were out walking around the shops by the harbor. I came across a stunning silver bracelet made by a local First Nations artist with orca designs around it. Andy said I was meant to have it as a symbol of protection and bought it for me as a Mother's Day gift. I just loved the synchronicity.

## Mystical Rainforest

I can see through the tall trees. Mist moves mysteriously through the greenery, beckoning me to follow. It leads me to the inner depths of a mystical rainforest. The soft needles of the cedar trees wave to me as the wind tickles their branches. Moss and ferns embellish the trail. There is a calmness in the air, it is sublime.

I spot a black-tailed deer beside a Douglas fir. He is the king of the forest, standing so strong, confident, handsome and wise. He wears his antlers with pride, his glare piercing the atmosphere. As our eyes meet, he becomes still as a statue. I capture this moment of splendor before he quickly disappears.

The salmon in the stream are abundant, swimming so freely. A truly magnificent wild wilderness. As I walk closer into the heavenly haze, I can hear the distant roar of a waterfall. It is mysterious and fierce just like you and me. A true reflection of the soul. Enter the mystery and recapture your essence.

## Tiny Wings

Gossamer wings of liberation, can you see? Witness me, if only for an instant. I am revealing myself to you in this rare moment. Don't look away, I have something to teach you. I may not have the wings of an Eagle, but my power is fierce.

I come to speak of creativity. I am locked so deep within you, but it's now time to free me. Release me into your welcoming embrace. Nurture these tiny wings for they will give you great flight into worlds you never thought were possible. Can you trust me?

## Thunder and Rain

Reflection of rain. Thunder from the sky paints my soul with every clap. Fire and desire in a rage of explosions. Thunderbolts echo through the woodland. Enchanted forest of mystery and myth, enter the flame of your flourishing gift. Old sage dressed in feathers, come share your stories.

Sapphire stone of blue, all this time it was you. Raindrops of ageless hue, your tenderness reminds me of all that is true. Blissfully blessing me and endlessly caressing me. Escape the maze of your heavenly haze.

## Two Hawks

This truly is God's country. I sometimes wonder why I would ever want to leave this idyllic place, filled with rivers, lakes and streams, snowcapped mountains, rainforests, glorious parks and rugged beaches. A place so rich with wildlife, bear, cougar, deer and magnificent eagles. This really is paradise.

I enter a deep meditation. Purple and sapphire expand throughout my body. There is a man in the distance. He is over six feet tall, but I can only make out his silhouette.

He begins talking to me in a deep, sincere tone, "I am from the northeast of Vancouver Island."

I immediately felt a hesitation go through my being, not sure if I was prepared for this encounter.

"Oh no, here we go again! Another instruction, another adventure, another wild chase of not knowing," I thought.

"You are protected," he reassures. "You are protected. Someone is waiting to meet you, but don't be afraid."

As I draw in another breath, he transforms into a bird of

prey, a hawk.

"My name is Two Hawks," he says, while cleaning my ears with his claw.

"But I only see one hawk?" I say to myself, my rational mind taking over to try and lure me out of the meditation.

The spirit hawk then begins cleaning my eyes with his wing to give me better eyesight. I begin to giggle like a child as he is tickling my face.

"You always come back to your focus," he explained, as a sudden gust of wind almost blows him away. "The wind may try to blow you in different directions, but you must remain focused and stay on your path. If you keep in your own lane and know where you are going, you will not be misled. You see, it is ourselves that are the worst tricksters of all. No one can deceive you as much as your own self."

"How true are his words?" I whispered to myself.

His gorgeous feathers were brushing over both my eyes as if to wipe away dust from them.

"There is an old whistle bone for you to collect," he tells me.

"Why must I gather this, and what does it mean?" I ask.

"It is very significant for this part of your life journey," he replies. "Have you forgotten how to trust?"

"Well things have become more difficult and challenging for me," I tell him.

"There are many other bones buried there, but only one is for you," he says. "This is an important symbol for your journey ahead."

"Why, am I preparing for death?" I ask.

"We are always preparing for our death," he answers. "We must always be ready as it comes when it wants to. Why do you fear death?"

"I don't fear death for myself," I reply, "but things are different since I became a mother. I must now be more practical and cautious."

"Caution will serve you at times throughout your life," he explains, "but for now you must enter the mystery once again."

"You mean the mystery I entered when I wrote my first book?" I enquire.

"Things have changed since then," he tells me, "and so have you. It is time."

In the distance I can hear wolves howling.

"Go and meet with the wolves," he says. "Can't you hear their spirits calling out to you?"

"Yes, Two Hawks, I always hear the spirit of the wolf call out to me because my soul is part of the pack."

Two Hawks flaps his wings and then turns into an elderly man, about seventy-five or eighty years old.

"You are ready to work this way now," he informs me. "You got the call to the island many years ago and now you will fully understand the importance. It's time to dance your dance. The Hawk will guide you and take you there, it's been a long time but your vision is back. The foresight you had many years ago has returned. Walk in balance, my friend, as balance walks with you. You wander between the worlds and are a messenger for many, as we are all messengers for one another. The problem arises when people don't pay attention. The Creator guides every single one of us on our journeys, but many find it too difficult to enter. If they would just be open to the idea that creation is always working for them, they will see the changes that can occur. Your world has become so fast like a whirlwind, spiraling through the existence of time. That is why it is so important now more than ever for everyone to learn their true identity. Many are fixated on money and poking into other people's business all the time. They should just stay focused on their own life. When they become a spirit traveler of the earth, everything will look different. Once they enter the portals of existence, there is no going back to the old ways, or the old self."

"But how do they do this, Two Hawks?" I ask.

"Once they recognize the importance of their presence in the world, they will understand how their very existence makes a difference," he says sweetly. "Conscious decisions will be made with coherent intentions. Remember that it is always down to a clear purpose, but all this can't work without self-love. What has become of your world is so much hatred, greed and competition. We are all one, and if all souls will acknowledge this, things will transpire. Be ready and be prepared, change is coming, the earth is moving too quickly. Give some tobacco and a piece of berry pie as an offering. The letters in the wind are coming to you."

"I don't understand, what does that mean?" I ask.

"Page-by-page you will finish this book," he explains. "We are the fathers, as the great father wolf in the sky we watch over you. Is it true you are a fatherless child?"

"Well yes, but all things have purpose even those things that are unexplained," I reply.

"You must trust more," he tells me. "You worry too much as a mother. This has changed many things for you but it has all been part of the teachings. A mother's and even a father's job is not to worry so much, but to be a teacher for your children. To nurture their hopes and dreams and help them walk with their fears. This will then continue for generations to come. Enter the great purple and blue sky with me now and grow gracefully into your own rightful place to serve and make a difference."

Shapeshifting back into a hawk once more, he spreads his wings.

"Hop onto my back," he suggests, "and be prepared for a great flight and to surrender any fears of entering another portal of existence. Are you ready?"

"Ready as I'll ever be," I declare.

I inhale deeply and see purple and sapphire enter my aura. I feel the new energy lifting my spirit into that of an eleven-year-old child. We are ascending higher and higher toward an opening through the clouds. A golden vortex, another portal to enter.

I tuck my head beneath the soft feathers of Two Hawks' shoulders. His wings feel muscular and sturdy; I am empowered. As we accelerate and speed through the golden aura portal, my body feels completely rejuvenated. I don't have a care in the world.

Two Hawks turns to look at me briefly. I can see his eyes more clearly now, they look wider. He knows who he is and nothing could alter his existence in this world. He is on a mission, with dedication and conviction, flying to wherever he is called.

He now expands into a giant hawk. I am but a tiny spec on his fluffy back. His feathers are darker and even softer. I feel so protected and trust him with all my heart.

Suddenly Two Hawks has vanished and I am back on Vancouver Island in the middle of a rainforest. It looks like Tofino. Such lush cedar, fir and spruce trees. They are the guardians of the forest. They know who they are. Nature knows how to stand firmly on the earth, embracing its uniqueness. It doesn't have to explain itself. How different the world would be if we were all true to nature like the trees in the wild rainforest, complementing one another and standing firmly together?

I am walking through the luscious forest, speaking to it, until it begins speaking to me. The fresh air and oxygen fill my lungs. I can breathe freely. I've never felt this much clean air go through my lungs before. I feel totally supported and watch the trees as they stand so proud and strong together. None of us should ever have to stand alone.

I can see a shadow behind one of the trees. It is a large wolf, almost giant like and very old. His image gradually fades away.

"The wolves protect the forest, they protect the bones," Two Hawks whispers from the spirit realm.

## Silver Birch Tree

In a meeting with a silver birch tree, I see my future self. I stand by the tree, leaning on it as if it is my best friend. I am in my seventies and look joyful and fulfilled. The wisdom of the tree, a reflection of the life I have lived. As I look through the eyes of my future self, she guides me through endless outcomes of what I can manifest for my life.

I invite you to come on another adventure with me. To the spirit of the silver birch tree. This sacred tree is a symbol of rebirth, protection and new beginnings. You are going to meet with your future self. An aspect of yourself that will show you all of the possibilities that you can create in your life.

Imagine that you are in a forest. You see the most beautiful silver birch tree calling out to you and you are immediately attracted to it. Put your hands on the tree and connect to its potent energy. Now sit with it and lean against its trunk. What does the energy feel like? This is a place of endless potential. Allow the spirit of the tree to support this exercise.

Imagine your future self meets you at the tree. What do you look like? Describe what you are wearing and what your persona is like. What do want to ask your future self and what advice do they have for you? This can be an emotional experience. Honor all the feelings that come up for you.

## The Eagle's Song

I watched the eagle from across the water, the sound of its song, so sweet. It is a young adolescent, still learning how to hunt and gather its food. The mother watches from above, perched on a branch high up in a cedar tree. There is no divide. Protective mother of all things, this is nature at its best, in its natural state. Creation's gift of song, perfectly in tune with the rhythm of the ocean's incoming tide. A divine, harmonious song in play.

The mother honors her young, blessing the journeys they will embark on together, and all of the pathways still to come.

Twice blessed by the great mother ocean in all her abundance, ever expansive and never without, as she is the mother of all.

Mother earth sustains and supports all of our journeys. Abundance is ours, within reach of our fingertips. Count your blessings each day. The stars are aligned, it is now your turn, for even if the blessings are never felt, still open your hands to receive.

As you set out on your path, you know where you are going. You have prepared for so many years for this very moment. Right now you have clear focus, clear vision, and immeasurable strength on your back, with such great power through your wings. Power and purpose to propel you in the direction your soul has already planned. You are being steered toward your destination, you earned this. Your mother now watches you from afar, as you carry her blessings with each flight on your grand adventure. May you glide effortlessly.

## Through the Eyes of an Eagle

Piercing through with clear vision. He glares at the sun without a blink, drinking from its rays, preparing for the day. He is a wizard in disguise, his long white hair and beard is part of the power that he carries.

Seeing what most people cannot, he carries messages from the spirit world and songs of liberation. He reaches the greatest heights in his flight. Never dare to stare in his eyes with lies. The truth cannot be hidden from this majestic being. He is fearless and the protector of nature.

## Chapter Fourteen

# The Cougar Waits at the Summit

Free is my heart, so still and serene, for the bitter pill no longer stings my being. I have climbed the steep slopes of this craggy mountain before, where souls are lost from the torment of the past. I have made it to the summit at last, but now in front of me stands a new mountain, a new day, a new dawn.

For the beauty of life is here, it has called to me. I have heard it deep down in my soul and tasted its sweet fragrance with my mouth that waters and yearns for more. I have danced with it, with love and pureness of being, with its grace within reach of my fingertips. Being alive here and now.

You see, life called to me, I did not call it. I am a spark in the darkness of night. I am in the stars, shining my inner glow throughout my being and into the horizon, beyond the limitless mind of sorrows and tomorrows. I am the gentle rain that refreshes and renews the earth. I am me. You are you. We are all refined masterpieces of divine beauty, beyond wonder.

Let's begin with the birth, not your infant birth but your rebirth. This new life that you have emerged from. 'Your real awakening.' Walking between the worlds has always been easy for me. Being able to communicate and be a seer of the otherworldly realm has always been a gift. Once perceived as a curse or misunderstood perhaps. Being looked at as strange is not as uncommon as one would think. Many people, especially teens, can relate to this. So, what you might believe is your greatest curse can often be your greatest gift.

We are all searching for freedom in one way or another, but freedom begins from within. So, the answer to everything that you are seeking is already inside of you. That might sound easy, but for many, it's not an easy thing at all.

"Cougar, my dear friend, I have made it to the peak."

"Yes, you have been very brave," replied my spirit animal. "You first saw me fifteen years ago on that dark road at night. You were mesmerized by the quickness of my leap as I pounced in front of your car. I have always known that you are not so much a lover of cats as you are of dogs, especially of course your spirit wolves. But you surrendered without judging me, and you have trusted me over these past long years."

"You have been good to me, my friend," I told him. "You have been teaching me about leadership, something I have had a difficult time with since I was a child. You are a good teacher, and I am so very grateful. Now that I have made it to the top of this mountain, you won't leave me, will you?"

"Of course not," he replied. "This journey has just begun as we have many more summits to climb. You have discovered things about yourself that you didn't realize were possible, and now you will go even deeper into your spiritual journey and reach even greater heights within yourself. There is so much more to the soul, it is a great mystery you know. We are all magical beings."

"You are a spirit animal, isn't it easier for you?" I asked.

"We all have our own journeys and so it is vital that we don't judge one another. We are each on our own personal discoveries, in our own time and at our own pace. The soul knows as it is eternal, and the physical body comprehends more than we give it credit for. That is why it is so important to take care of your vehicle. You only have one body to last you a lifetime, and so it must be nourished, nurtured, and deeply listened to. Too many people don't listen to their bodies. Did you know that the secrets and mysteries are also held within the body? You must take care of it for yourself, your family and all those you have chosen to serve."

## The Lake Freezes Over

Frozen, your life is still. Silent, a time of contemplation. A life review of all things big and small, all those things that shook you to the core and made you freeze. Your memory is at a pause. So cold, you held the blanket so tight. Chilled to the bone, you sought warmth from your child spirit that lit the flame within to keep you alive. The fire was extinguished when the ice began to melt, melting away the memories. They faded along with the embers that burned from deep within your soul.

It was time for a rebirth, a long-awaited renewal of spirit. The aurora borealis shone through my essence, my soul nudged by the vibrant colors. I punched the ice with my fist and it fractured. My anger had cracked open the frozen lake of pain. I broke through the weakened ice, melting the icicles still clinging to my shattered heart from all the tears of pain and shame.

At the bottom of the lake was a butterfly, frozen in time, waiting for resurrection in the spring when the birds will sing and welcome me back from a long, cold sleep. The flowers will begin to bloom so I can inhale and ingest the sweet fragrance of life, once again.

I have been given another chance to begin something new. Somewhere in the meadow of my soul, the wildflowers are free. I am liberated. I stood in the freezing cold long enough to feel the discomfort and the pain, frozen like the lake and the memories. I recaptured a glimpse of them, but not to relive the pain, to release it out of my body that no longer represents that lake. The lake of pain is now gone forever. I am grateful for it has been a good teacher, one that enabled me to finally live again.

## Lake Louise

The calling to visit Lake Louise was so strong I had no choice but to listen. This is one of my favorite places in all of Canada, the energy is so clean and pure. It is a portal entry for Archangel

Michael, and his energy can be strongly felt. I set up a meeting at one of the hotels to view as a potential venue for a future retreat I was planning to teach here. The last time I had visited was on another family road trip with Andy and the kids.

The flight from Nanaimo was just under two hours into Calgary. I picked up a rental car and drove to Banff where I was staying. I could already sense the energy I would be entering. It was lighter, and a good break from the Island where the energies were starting to feel heavier. My soul was in need a boost.

The spirit of my wolf pack was strongly guiding this journey. Signs of this became even more clear when I ended up staying at the Studio Wolf Condo. I loved the synchronicity and gave a huge smile to my pack upon entering the room. It was perfect with a wood-burning fireplace to keep me cozy and warm. There was a picture of a grey wolf hanging on the wall which made the room feel even more welcoming, and another gorgeous wolf picture hanging above my bed. I felt so blessed to be reminded of my animal spirit guides who are constantly reassuring me of their presence.

This was a perfect writing getaway and a chance for me to complete more of this book. I settled in and rested for the night. I dreamed I was walking down a hallway and was ready to open a new door where my pack of wolves greeted me, brushing against my legs and kissing my nose and ears.

I awoke the next morning to a cool, crisp spring day. The drive to Lake Louise was only thirty-five minutes. I parked the car and walked to the lake which was completely frozen. There were lots of tourists walking on it, capturing the majestic winter scenery. I sat on a bench waiting for some of the people to leave before entering the lake. It resembled a scene from a Christmas card.

I could feel the vortex energy and my solar plexus expanding along with my third eye chakra. My whole body was becoming lighter. All the stress I had stored was leaving my body and I visualized my cells and organs becoming healthier. I heard the word 'regeneration'. There was another healing opportunity at this portal.

Every time we visit a sacred site and enter an energy vortex, we progress on our spiritual and individual paths. It is important not to attempt to bypass this spiritual journey. We have the support of the earth's energies while we move through our own individual healing. For my own journey, this has assisted me greatly by offering a gentler energy while I traversed through some deep, dark terrain.

I always welcome the dynamic essence of Archangel Michael. He was here to assist me on yet another transformation of my mind, body and spirit. I looked out to the frozen lake as more people started to leave. My eye caught an ethereal blue energy expanding through what appeared from my viewpoint to be a pyramid at the end of the lake. At the center of the pyramid, an electric blue light was expanding upwards from the bottom, all the way to the tip. I intuitively knew this was Michael's spirit.

As a few more tourists left, I was now ready to enter through the vortex and on to the frozen lake. I thanked Michael with every step and every breath. I walked out to the center of the lake and paused. The sun's rays were radiating through me.

With the vision of my third eye, I could see the magnetic blue energy passing from the bottom of my feet right through my body. I could feel it recharging my energy field as it moved through all of my chakras. I experienced a cleansing and a renewal of electric energy. I had entered a portal of serene solitude. I stood there, basking in this activation through my essence.

The image of a seal spirit animal came to meet with me. I imagined we were swimming with such grace through the lake. It then connected to the sea in Ammassalik, Greenland, a special place I visited many years ago and wrote about in my first book *Awakening the Divine Soul: Finding Your Life Purpose*. The seal was blessing me with a memory from the spirits of that land. It was also reminding me to be more playful in my life and to keep expanding my imagination.

I drew in a breath as if I was back in Greenland for a moment. My power animal and I were swimming through the sea with feelings of pure liberation. I felt cleansed by the water once again, and sent my love to the spirit of the elders and the land I had connected with all those years ago.

My energy was now being brought back to the vortex at Lake Louise. I was grounded in a big ball of gold and blue light. I sent the light out to the spirits of the land and thanked them once again for the reconnection. I felt the firm ice underneath my feet and the strength coming from the lake.

In my mind's eye I could see gorgeous green and blue colors underneath the ice and felt the protection of the lake. I took in a deep breath while electric blue and white energies continued expanding through the top of the pyramid. I imagined Archangel Michael's hands were radiating even more light. His palms were facing toward the lake and he was directing the light toward me like a laser shining straight through my heart. As the vibration of the light expanded through my whole body, I inhaled again, feeling completely revitalized.

Another spontaneous healing took place as it started to snow. I looked up at the sky to capture the snowflakes as they gently caressed my face.

I heard bells ringing outside of the hotel next to the lake. It was time for lunch.

## Enter the Portal

Pause for a moment and take in a deep breath. Visualize that you are at Lake Louise. What does it feel like to be here? Quiet your thoughts by focusing on your breath. Imagine that you are entering a new portal. Invite the rays of the sun to move through every part of your being. Now visualize a vibrant, blue light in front of you. Breathe it in as you enter into a new vibration of this higher frequency. Invite the essence of Archangel Michael to join you. What does his energy feel like?

Be open to receiving any messages you receive through your creative visualization. Expand into your intuitive imagination without judgement. Everything you encounter is relevant. Honor the unique journey that is yours. Write down your experience and give thanks to the spirit of Lake Louise and Archangel Michael. You may want to reach for crayons, colored pencils or paint to draw your experience or the energy that you are feeling.

## Grizzly Bears

I was so excited to be meeting my friend Jolynn for lunch. I hadn't seen her since our trip in Arizona. We had booked the gorgeous restaurant overlooking Lake Louise, and sat down at a table overlooking the majestic glacier with the most spectacular view of the lake. I felt like I was still in a powerful portal, and immediately reached for my pen and notepad to capture the creative writing ideas that were flowing through so abundantly.

I was now well grounded after a delicious, light lunch. Jolynn and I had some appointments to visit some other hotels to look at their space. We were planning to collaborate and host a spring workshop after the writing retreat I was looking to teach in the autumn.

On our way there, we saw many cars pulling in at the side of the road. Something was going on, so I asked Jolynn to pull over. What a magnificent sight it was. Right in front of us was a mother grizzly bear and her two cubs. This was such a rare sight. We were in the right place at the most divine timing.

This was one of the most beautiful sights of nature's gift I have ever witnessed. We watched as the mother bear rubbed her back against a pole while the baby cubs were curiously playing. After a while, people started getting too close to the bears and so the police were called to scare them away with their sirens. We thanked the spirit of the bears for this blessing.

## A Herd of Elk

I was heading back to my hotel, happy for the time I had spent with my dear friend. I noticed I was getting low on gas so I stopped at the nearest station to fill up. My intuition was strongly telling me to head back in the opposite direction. I brushed it off a couple of times until the nudge was so strong, I decided to listen to the guidance and turn around. It didn't make any rational sense as I was going the wrong way. It would soon be dark, and I still had to drive back to Banff.

After a short while, I was rewarded with the most magnificent sight, a huge herd of elk. They were everywhere, another blessing from the Universe. I was so glad I listened to that voice within and followed my intuition. I have never seen that many elk before. I was able to capture some incredible photos and video footage, and felt exhilarated. The spirit of the elk was so very abundant.

When the spirit of the elk appears, it can be a sign and confirmation that we are going in the right direction. Another lesson was learned to always listen to that inner voice, the deep whisper from your higher knowledge. Stand tall with confidence, listen to the wisdom but also know the boundaries. For me personally, it was all about putting up boundaries, something I wasn't too good at but finally got the message loud and clear. The elk taught me to go more inward to respect my deeper sense of self without shame or limitations, honoring my greater purpose in life.

## Tending the Fire

My heart was still wide open after the healing at Lake Louise. I knew that my physical body would be playing catch up with my vibrational body, yet again, to match the new frequencies that had been activated within me. This connection with the fire was a huge healing experience that lasted for almost seven hours. It was a real time of forgiveness and grief. My heart was releasing so much.

The unwavering spirit of the fire was there for me. I sobbed and sobbed until my heart couldn't take any more. It was a rawness that only the element of fire has witnessed. My companion, my faithful friend holding space for me and giving me the courage to release the stagnant pain. It was time to move on. I had no choice but to surrender to the spirit of fire that held my every secret within its flames, slaying the past and accompanying memories. It gave me warmth and comforted me while I became its companion. I began to understand what it needed to unite, to merge and to continue, by expanding the flames of its creation.

The flames keep burning if you continue to feed the fire. Your passion needs to be nurtured. If you don't continue to tend the fire, it will burn out. Tending the fire requires a sharp eye, an open heart and a knowing of when the flame will go out. What do you need in your life right now to tend to the sacred fire within? How will you see to your burning desire? Can you handle the deep passion, or will you explore a reckless path?

If you watch the logs burning in a fireplace, you will come to understand the natural rhythm. I looked out of the window for a moment. As fresh flakes fell, it looked like a winter wonderland, a snowy fairy tale. I was now in a small cabin in Emerald Lake for the night. It was the first time I had to keep a fire going by myself. It was such a powerful experience. There truly is an art to it, or at least that's what I was taught by the spirit of the fire during those seven hours. I sat with the flames as they kept my room warm.

Pause for a moment. Be still and take in a deep breath. Move into your creative visualization and imagine a fire burning and that you are the only person tending to it. You have an opportunity to learn from the element of fire. Are you ready to let go and release something? What will you let go of? Now enter the world of inspiration. Think of something that inspires you and breathe it in three times.

Sit quietly with the fire of your imagination and your deep passion. Let it wander, do not judge where it takes you. Feel the essence of your creativity and bless it, even if you don't quite understand what it means. It will all make sense to you as you continue to feed the flames of your passion. The dreams you thought were long forgotten will return to serenade you with the sweetest songs. Your brow chakra is expanding into those forgotten dreams where your intuition comes to life.

## Dancing Fearlessly in the Fire

Imagine you are merging your passion into a fiery dance, knowing that the fire is your friend. Continue to sit with the flames and focus on your intention. What are you most deeply passionate about? Ask one of your power animals to join you. Who appears?

Breathe into a deeper connection with your spirit ally. What are they showing you, do they have something to share? Imagine you are dancing fearlessly. Detach from any expectations or outcomes and release your free spirit.

Feel the heat of the fire as your passion rises. Feel your body moving as your creative juices continue to flow through you. See your arms and legs moving into a divine dance. Is your power animal dancing with you? This exercise will help you to feel liberated and release any stagnant energy with support from the fire spirit. Go with the flow and thank the element of fire for supporting your journey of empowerment.

## Emerald Lake

You stand between two worlds where they collide. There is complete stillness when a mysterious mist enters the scene.

You breathe with the earth into one heartbeat as the crisp air becomes your breath. Its mystery speaks to you. You are one with creation as all things merge. The green waters of forgiveness, the forbidden waters of imagination.

Push through, break free from the limitations that burden you, keeping you from your true essence. The wild spirit within longs to be free and return to self. Release the echoes of the past, free at last. You have forgiven yourself from the harshness that was preserved deep inside your core. The cold winter lives on inside your body, still frozen within the cold waters of judgement. Chilled to the bone, now soften your breath and release the tension that has paralyzed you from within, spreading ice throughout your world.

As the soft spirit of the fresh wind comes to kiss your face, do not be afraid. Open your heart to the sun as it reflects off the Emerald Lake. All reflections of you, the lake of your dreams. Now let go, let it all go. As the ice melts so does any remaining bitterness, while the green waters flow into your heart. Your dreams come to life, so make space for new memories. Fresh snow begins to fall, tickling every part of you, a sign of renewal as the wolf howls its sovereignty.

# Chapter Fifteen

# Become the Mystery

You are the mystery, a gift waiting to be unwrapped. Search deeper within your sacred temple. Pause for a moment and take in a deep breath of renewal. Exhale what you think your life should be at this very moment. Detach yourself from any expectations or outcomes. Start fresh, right here and now.

You have come so far into this book and on your own unique, sacred journey of rebirth and renewal. I am so grateful to be sharing this magical journey with you. There is infinitely more to you, more than you can ever imagine. Continue allowing it all to unfold. You are the great mystery waiting to emerge into your divine life, as you recreate and manifest the journey of your deepest desires.

Keep your pilot light lit, and the flame of your existence burning strong. May your passion be ignited into the sacred flame of eternity. I invite you to come on a deeper meditation to that place of mystery within that has not yet revealed itself. Let go of all opinions and judgements.

Focus on the flame that you have ignited, burning deep within the very core of you. Visualize it expanding within your belly and then spreading throughout your whole being. Be aware of your body and move into the stillness of just being present. Breathe in gratitude for your life, all of your experiences, and for making it this far on your courageous journey.

Throughout your imagination there is always a veil. Visualize it in front of you. What color is it? What fabric is it made of? Reach out your arms to touch it. How does it make you feel? What does it remind you of? Take in another deep breath as you connect to your intuition. Are you ready to lift the veil into your new life? If so, go ahead and lift it.

If it doesn't feel right for you at this moment, sit with it and give yourself permission to receive the wisdom. Don't judge whether you are ready or not. Your intuition will always guide you. There is no greater teacher than yourself. Only you know the truth and will have crystal clear clarity if this is the right time. Everything happens in divine timing, so trust this to be true. If you have lifted the veil, breathe in the new energy you have entered and invite this new vibration into your life.

Take in another deep breath and exhale the old vibration of what no longer serves you. What word comes up for you? Write down the word that represents the old you. Draw in yet another breath. You will see a different word that represents the new energy. Write it down. As you sit with the word, be aware of what color you see within your new frequency. If this feels right for you, expand your breath and extend this color throughout your whole body and expand the vibration throughout your being. Give yourself some time to adjust to this new energy.

## Intuitive Imagination

Your imagination is your intuition. This is your natural state. When you were a child, you were always using your intuition because your imagination was your real world. As we grow older, we move away from the world of make-believe and step more into our rational thinking. It is good to have a balance, but also important that you don't completely lose your natural state of being. It is when we start to care too much about what others will think of us, that our clear intuition gets clouded. This can happen during adolescence, as I have witnessed many times. There are no limitations to the world of imagination.

Do you remember all those adventures you went on as a child? Invite back the magical world of wonder. As you do this you will find your intuition will be heightened. Once we start to do the inner work on ourselves, we invite it back. That is when the real transformation happens. We then move into manifestation. I have manifested and witnessed incredible things in my life through accessing my intuitive imagination. It truly is a place of divine wonder. Doors will start to open for you once you are in divine alignment and in the flow of oneness with your imagination.

## Clean Slate

The way ahead is clear for you to see. Where will you walk to? In what direction will you go? You have the power to choose a new path. Are you ready to wipe the slate clean and embrace and celebrate your journey of rebirth and renewal? Be still for ten minutes or however long you wish to remain motionless in silence. Bask in the energy of stillness and breathe.

## Grandfather Trees Standing Tall

The ancient men of honor, standing tall and free. They are not afraid to be gentle, they have surrendered their fierceness and their armor. They have dignity and wisdom to share. No longer at battle, they are now at peace. Their love radiates as it touches the sky.

Walk between these trees and you will be blessed. They will teach you of nobility. They have been through many storms, but their roots remain strong. They removed their protective battle attire and stand naked and exposed, but still protect the forest.

There are sacred waterfalls within this woodland. The rejuvenating waters can restore you in every way imaginable. Something magical is happening. Bathe in the secret pools of this revered place and make a wish. Let the healing waters touch every part of you. Your deepest desires are now flowing to a place that goes through eternity.

The Goddess of the forest stands tall with the grandfathers, her long golden hair blowing freely in the wind. She wears a white dress laced with golden thread. Call to her and she will meet you wherever you are within yourself. She reflects your authentic self back to you. She is a mirror showing you exactly what you need to see.

## The Gathering of Black Wolves

I enter the journey. Twelve black wolves are surrounding me.

"Come, I invite you to enter, but only through the eyes of the wolves," said the alpha male.

"What do you mean?" I asked.

"Enter through the eyes of the wolves," he repeated.

I stood there for a moment with a puzzled look on my face. I looked around at all of the other wolves. Their fur was so shiny and their eyes pierced through my soul. I understood what he meant, he wanted me to shapeshift into a wolf and join them. I knew how to do this and had done it before throughout my years of shamanic journeying.

I love merging with my spirit animals. It has always been a beautiful and empowering experience. I knew this gathering was being arranged to show me something important, and felt safe amongst these magnificent beings of beauty.

The black wolves were encouraging me to walk with them so they could support and witness every inch of my journey. The alpha came forward, sniffing me as he got closer.

"This is a crucial meeting about standing out, showing your vulnerabilities, coming out of your den, and letting the world know who you are," he told me.

This made me feel a little uncomfortable. I had become so used to staying snug inside my den for many years now, raising my three kids and writing my books.

The alpha continued, "With all your gifts and all of your flaws, it's time for you to expose all that you are, especially to yourself first. Those tiny steps out of the den and into the wide Universe are needed for all of us, particularly in these times of great change in our world."

I looked at each of the wolves that still surrounded me. It

was a glorious sight to see the contrast of their gleaming black fur against the backdrop of the snowy, white landscape. Their amber eyes glowing as if the sun was radiating right through them. They stood out so clearly, and I now realized what he was explaining. I was still uncomfortable, however, as the thought scared me and I just wanted to run back inside my den, but I also knew it was time for me to step outside of my comfort zone. I have had to do this often throughout my life and was now ready once again.

I heard the wind howling in the distance, getting closer to us. The snow started blowing all around us in a sudden blizzard, but I could still make out the silhouettes of the wolves like dark shadows in a mysterious painting. Their stunning golden eyes glaring at me, telepathically guiding me to follow. I felt energized.

The wolves began howling in perfect harmony with the wind. It was haunting but incredibly empowering. The new moon peeked out from behind the fast-moving clouds for a moment. I enjoyed a brief glimpse of her, knowing this was a sign of new beginnings. I lifted my head, holding it higher than ever before in complete trust, and ran off through the snowy wilderness with my power animals on a new adventure.

## The Enchanted Forest

In the place where all things are possible, you enter the world of your deepest and wildest imagination. Things come to life here in natural play and your dreams become real. Negative aspects of your thoughts are put under a spell to cast away any remaining shadows blocking your radiance. The chase is over. This is the place to dream, where you capture your true identity.

Enter the ambiance of deep purple, sapphire and magenta as they intertwine through the enchanted forest. Invite these colors to empower you and to realign your path. As night falls, fireflies light up the pathway, dancing all around you.

Do you believe in this place? Reach deeper into your imagination and bring it to life. Reach for your journal and write down your experience. You might like to draw or paint a picture of your very own enchanted forest.

## The White Spirit Stag

It was two o'clock in the morning and my heart was thumping like a drum. It felt as if someone was pounding my chest with a beater. I was drifting in and out of the dream state. I was experiencing a mild anxiety attack. Oh yes, that feeling was all too familiar. I was entering the zone and something very exciting was about to happen. I call it the zone because it's a place where all things exist. There is no concept of time or space and everything is at a parallel reality.

My white spirit Stag suddenly appeared. He has come to me a couple of times in shamanic journeys, but never in the dreamtime. He only comes to see me when the veil between the worlds is thin. He is bold and beautiful with such strength, and yet a presence of elegance and grace.

I climbed onto his back and noticed he had a book in his mouth. It was the color sapphire and had my name written on it. He was showing me that it was time to complete my next book. I told him that I wanted to see it, but it disappeared from his mouth and reappeared in an eagle's nest. A bald Eagle now had my book in its mouth. I trusted that I would see it when the time was right. I had three or four different manuscripts on the go at the time, so I wasn't sure which book he was trying to show me.

The white Stag then took me into a garden. There were so many gorgeous flowers and I inhaled their sweet aroma. An exquisite white and purple orchid caught my attention. I walked over to sit with her and felt the softness of her petals. The orchid has always been my favorite flower. As I looked at her more closely, admiring her beauty, I smiled at her and got the sense that she smiled back at me. I drifted off back into a deep sleep.

## Grandfather Wolf

"He has stepped out of the shadow, he has returned," I thought to myself.

So calm, consoling and affectionate, he came to comfort me, but what I didn't realize was that he was there all along. From the moment I came out of the birth canal, he waited to greet me, to honor and celebrate me. The great howls of creation blessed me into the wolf dance of existence. My life was to be whatever I chose it to be, but this would take time, many years in fact, and sometimes seem like a never-ending arduous path.

My wolf clan came and held me to see me through the initiation of creation. My dear grandfather wolf is a giant. The biggest wolf I have ever seen, and the great protector of time. He told me my purpose here on this great landscaped wilderness is to explore. He taught me to see more clearly, to find my voice, and to really howl. He told me I must learn how to re-wild myself, to become undone from ways that did not serve me.

All the things I thought I had been, have disappeared deep through the mist of the forest. He met me on the moonlit trail that forever changed the course of my life. The endless woods with trees that kiss the sky. The forest of wisdom is now my home, as I sit under an old oak tree. The roots and branches are solid, filled with ancient wisdom, just like him. I curl up beside him, my arms wrapped around his giant body. His fur is aged but still soft. My head nestled under his ear, I lay down to rest and slip into another deep dreamtime. I am protected, as he is the gatekeeper of many things. I feel loved, so deeply loved.

## Snowy Owl Medicine

It felt like a blizzard was on the way. The snow was falling heavily, and it was hard to see what was in front of me. I instinctively knew the igloo was not far away, so I kept going. As the wind picked up, I covered part of my face with a purple and lilac woolen scarf, with matching gloves that kept my hands warm.

I finally made it. I entered the igloo but where were my spirit parents? I was all alone with only a carpet made from polar bear fur to sit on.

"Time for contemplation," I heard my spirit mother's voice whisper.

I sat down on the bearskin rug in the stillness. The igloo felt warm after the harsh wintry storm outside. It was wonderful to return to myself. I had completed this journey and come back full circle. I had followed my teacher's advice to complete the circle and finish the book.

I looked down at the lilac pouch that was around my neck. I removed my gloves and held it in my hands, stroking the soft white wolf fur with my fingers. I remembered my guides telling me to access it whenever I needed to. I wanted to ask if there was anything else to go into the book before it came to completion.

I opened the pouch and pulled out a white snowy owl feather. As I held it, I remembered the powerful dream I had over twenty years ago, where a white owl spirit had helped me through the fear of surgery before I had a lymph node removed. Years later, the events in that dream came true in the exact sequence I had dreamt them, when I had the opportunity to visit beautiful Boundary Bay in British Columbia. It is just a ferry ride away from where I was living on Vancouver Island, and I'd heard that snowy owls return here at the same time every year. They congregate on the marshlands of Boundary Bay, using it as a stopping off point during their migration south for the winter. It is a photographer's dream to capture images of these incredible birds. It was breathtaking to see all of the stunning owls perched on logs and old tree stumps.

I reconnected with the spirit of my snowy owl and thanked her again for staying with me all these years. She is still one of my dearest spirit animals and I am truly grateful.

Call upon the spirit of the snowy owl when you want to

connect with higher knowledge, protection, and seeing beyond illusion. Power animals have various meanings and symbols in different cultures. You will understand your personal connection to your spirit animal more clearly by building a deeper relationship with them. In my experience, my various power animals come to assist me in different areas in my life. This is an individual and very personal journey between you and them.

## Chapter Sixteen

# Enter the Dance

Spiral vortex of colors moving through the atmosphere into a temple of light. Spinning through a portal of oneness. I invite you to enter the dance. Walk through the doors of the temple to see more clearly and feel the energy in all its abundance. Let the pretty colors speak to you as you access an endless portal of creation.

Feel each one as the seasons pass through your soul. Look down at your feet and hands as you dance. See all the mystical hues moving within you. Now enter the garden of magical flowers. They are ready to bloom. Dance with their spirit. Are you ready to emerge and blossom in all the unexpected places within your being? Rise up and keep on dancing.

### Didgeridoo Dance

I could hear a soft voice speaking to me, "Come, child, come, he is waiting for your healing."

I knew it was Lia.

"Where are you, Lia?" I called out.

I couldn't see her but could sense her spirit was close. An Indigenous Australian man appeared, his face painted black and white. There were lines going across his cheeks, the upper line was painted white, the middle was black and the lower was white. I couldn't see a clear image, it was more of a silhouette. He looked to be about five and a half feet tall.

He spoke to me in a firm tone, "Step back into the dreamtime, it has been so long. You have forsaken it for too long now. Put these rocks under your pillow and enter the dream world once again. Be more still, your mind has become busy with many chores. You are mothering your children, but you must also mother yourself and let your creativity spring forth."

I remembered the stones that I bought when I travelled to Australia. I was living in England at the time and used to put them under my pillow. They were now sitting on my bookshelf. I moved into a deeper state of relaxation. I began focusing on my breathing and entered the journey.

I was standing on the red earth. My feet were bare and the man was playing a didgeridoo over them. To my right side I could see the words 'old me'. It was a disturbing image as the letters were made of flesh with maggots eating away at them. I turned my head away but understood the message. The old me was dying. Everything about how I had been living my life was fading away, old attachments, old judgements, old vibrations, they were all coming to an end. There had to be the death of the 'old me' in order to welcome the rebirthing process for the 'new me'.

He told me to focus my energy on the earth beneath my feet. I felt the vibrations from the earth merging and dancing, twirling in synch with the sounds of the didgeridoo. There were rainbow colors moving through my feet and all the way up through my entire being. My body began vibrating just like the instrument. I could feel the old energy leaving me. The self-doubt, low self-esteem, and unworthiness were all melting away.

It was the final stages of everything I had prepared for during the many years of my healing journey. Even the areas where I had been retriggered. I didn't realize there was so much of it still inside of me. I breathed into it and began to tremble. I continued to breathe deeply as the haunting sounds of the didgeridoo echoed throughout all of my cells and every fiber of my being.

The kind man looked into my eyes and moved the instrument away from his mouth.

"Look up at the sky," he said.

I could now see his beautiful face more clearly. His smile

reflected the warmth coming from his eyes which, in turn, mirrored his soul. I looked up to see the most spectacular sunset. Crimson, purple, orange and yellow painted the sky in an auspicious array.

"Wow," I murmured.

I drew in another breath feeling fully present with nature's divine gift. At that very moment, I could feel something touch the middle of my back, just beneath my shoulder blades. It was the end of the didgeridoo. Once again, I felt the vibrations of the sound waves playing through me. I surrendered and became still. I could feel the stagnant energy and all of the pain, particularly in my lower back, being released from my body.

"Balance," he said, as his lips moved away from the mouthpiece of the profoundly healing instrument. "It's all about balance," his tone had changed, it was softer now. "It's time to find a new equilibrium and a new way of being if you are to fulfil your purpose here on the earth at this time. Our planet is changing and we must begin with ourselves."

I looked into his eyes; the love and compassion radiating from him was undeniable. It was a clear reflection of his beautiful soul. I thanked him with all of my heart for supporting me on my journey. I sensed a deep trust with him and felt blessed that another helper in the spirit world was now assisting me.

We often stand in our own way of healing. There is a reluctance to move forward, perhaps it is fear of the unknown. Sometimes it's easier to stay in our comfort zone than to take a risk or to step forward and trust. We know when certain parts of our lives aren't working anymore, but we have a tendency to stay in jobs that we are no longer fulfilled in, for the financial security. We also stay in friendships and relationships that we are aware no longer serve us, for fear of being alone or out of loyalty.

There comes a time in our lives when we can no longer hide the truth about how we are feeling. Ignoring the truth will only keep us from the liberating life that is ahead. What do you think is holding you back? Most of the time this is fear, and that very fear can become our self-imposed prison. We all have the courage inside us to make the decisions needed to live a more fulfilling and joyful life.

You may notice a part of yourself dying. It could be your passion or just the zest for life you once had. What part of yourself are you willing to let go of in order to prepare for your rebirth? What would renewal look like for you? Are you ready to make the changes to move into the life you want to manifest for yourself?

## Mystic Dance

Close your eyes and take a deep breath. Be fully present with your beautiful body. Imagine that your feet are firmly planted on the red earth. Take in another breath and visualize yourself walking barefoot. You can feel the support of mother earth as you take each step. If you were to have balance in your life, what would that look like for you?

Now respectfully invite this wonderful guide to play the didgeridoo over your feet. You might see, sense, hear or feel his presence. Use your imagination and don't judge the encounter, just be in the moment. Everything you experience is relevant. See yourself moving your feet into a sacred, mystical dance that is the greatest expression of yourself. Extend your arms out and move your whole body into your own natural rhythm. Breathe in deeply and expand your breath out into the world.

If it feels right for you, expand on the dance from your vision by standing up and physically moving into your mystic dance. This will bestow even more power by heightening your imagination through physical movements. It is also a good idea to have a journal close by to write down your experience. I highly encourage logging all of the exploits you have, so you may reflect on them at another time. You will be amazed at how much wisdom is in these written words.

## Re-creating the Dream

Your dream is waiting within the vibrant colors of the majestic sunset. It is in the clear, crystal waterfall and the swirling northern lights. Breathe it into your being and give birth to your vibrant creation. Your dream is the naked, first cry of a newborn, waiting to be cradled, nurtured and loved.

You recreate your dream with support from the four seasons. It is in every winter snowflake, every drop of spring rain, in the autumn leaves and the summer sunshine. Your dream is in the wildflowers that blossom so magnificently, and in the caterpillar that waits inside the cocoon to transform into a majestic butterfly. Your dream will morph into all the splendid colors of the rainbow.

## The Dreamer's Stone

"That was an incredible dance, Lia," I said while catching my breath.

"You must continue to work with the dreamer's stone," she advised.

"Which one?" I asked.

"The white and purple," she replied.

"That's my favorite," I thought to myself.

"It's not by chance or accident that certain people come into your life, all is relevant," she explained. "Everyone you meet is a teacher, even when it feels far from it. You must learn the lessons, learn them with grace. You have done this, child, there is so much you humans go through, but to feel is a gift, don't see it as a curse. To be in touch with the deepest parts of yourself is a real blessing. You mustn't get ahead of yourself, take one step at a time, and remember, you need to have balance. Savor the moments, stay in them to fully connect with the feeling."

I looked up at Lia with the innocent eyes of a young child,

admiring her wisdom. I loved my meetings with her. I smiled and she smiled back at me. I noticed she was wearing white and yellow, just like when we first met.

"You look a little different, Lia," I said to her.

"So do you, child, I think we both look brighter," she replied with an even bigger smile on her face.

"I think so too," I said.

She leant over to kiss my forehead and then wiped clean my brow chakra, my third eye.

"Always remember to clean this area," she informed me. "You pick up so much of other people's energies that it's important you continue to do this."

I thanked her and gave her a big hug. I felt the strength she was blessing me with for my new journey. I noticed the moon becoming so bright, it was full with a clear sky. We both admired her beauty.

"The spirit of the moon will always guide you on your pathways," she told me. "Pay attention to her cycles as they affect your physical body. You all came here to remember who you are. We all come from the stars, we are the people from forever."

As we continued to connect with the spirit of the moon, there were so many meteorites and shooting stars darting across the night sky. With each one we saw, I felt the vibrations empower my body like they were recharging me with energy. I saw myself dancing back in the circle again. Lia reached for my hand and then disappeared. I laid still as the beat of the drum brought me back from this unbelievable journey. I breathed in gratitude.

## Chapter Seventeen

# Rebirth

I entered my meditation room to see that the sun's rays were radiating the most gorgeous rainbow colors through the crystals hanging from my window. What a wonderful way to start my meditation.

I saw an image of the golden egg my teacher had gifted me at the juniper tree in Boynton Canyon, Sedona. It was in my hands and ready to hatch! Cracks on the sides of the egg were becoming visible. It felt so real, something was emerging from the egg. Suddenly the head of a baby eagle broke through the shell. It pushed its body free and began growing and growing until it was now a giant golden eagle, its wings were huge.

I intuitively knew this was a symbol for protection, rebirth and renewal. It was a protector of all things and a messenger for all beings. It was stunning, pure elegance. I watched with amazement as it flew up into the sky in an incredible flight of splendor straight into the sun. This moment of magnificence completely took my breath away.

### The Mystic Tree

My meditation took me to an unusual type of tree that I didn't recognize. My guides told me it can be wherever you want it to be. It is both male and female. It is strong and in perfect balance. Anyone can visit this tree whenever they want to. It will call to you at the most divine times.

This tree is where magic happens. It changes color like a chameleon, depending on what vibration you are in. This sacred tree exists only in your imagination. It will nurture you, comfort you and reenergize you when you are feeling depleted. Look at the branches. They represent an extension of you. They reach out and keep growing as you do.

I looked up to see my golden eagle perched at the very top of the mystic tree. The spirit of the tree suddenly became even more alive. Imagine you too can see the eagle. Watch it and feel its magnificent energy. What is the golden eagle's message for you? Write down your experience at your very own mystic tree. You may like to draw, color or paint a picture of what your tree looks like. Describe what it means to you.

## Spirit Bear and Wolf Mountain

The spirit of all things is constantly listening to and guiding us. We are interconnected to everything. One night I was praying for a getaway, a place where I could go to finally finish this book. It had been a while since I was in my own space to write. The kids were doing well, embracing their own creativity and passions while Andy and I continued to support them on their individual journeys. Our family life was still very busy.

I felt the soul of this book tugging at my sacral chakra. I knew the time was right and soon it would be complete. Andy and I are total opposites, I am Libra and he is Aries. Our energies were constantly clashing, so I felt the time away would be good for us both.

The very next morning a gorgeous resort within British Columbia became available at a great price. It was Spirit Ridge at the Nk'Mip Resort in the sacred desert land of the Osoyoos Indian band. My dear friend Layla was also wanting to get away for a retreat. Her birthday was coming up so I booked it for the two of us. It was such great timing for both of us.

As I loaded up the car, the spirit of this place was already calling to me, and I knew it would be the perfect getaway. It was a five-hour drive from Vancouver up through the snowy mountains, but I trusted that my spirit allies had my back. When you pray with intention, with all your being, the Universe will always back you up. With deep faith I took the journey.

What I didn't expect was the rich and abundant land that I was to walk upon. The sacred land of the people of the Okanagan. The closer I got to Spirit Mountain, the more my heart began to feel an expansion of love and serenity. This feeling was nothing I had ever experienced before in all the years I've lived in British Columbia. There were no words to define the overwhelming peace within my whole being. I was home, back to nature, into the wilderness.

When we open ourselves up to the unknown and deeply trust, we will be taken to places that we have never imagined. A place back to the heart and soul of who we are. That natural state of oneness with all of creation. What I experienced nestled amongst the desert, the mountains, and the vineyards was a true empowerment journey of the heart. Nature will always emancipate us, so stay open to receiving the blessings that are waiting for you.

During my time at Spirit Mountain, I gained even more clarity about my life. I felt unshackled and ready to move forward on my continuing journey of the soul. Everything was becoming clearer, and my heart was opening again after a challenging period in my marriage.

I was feeling grateful for all the amazing inner child work I had done over the years. I was having even more breakthroughs in areas of my life that could not have healed without my precious three children mirroring back to me the things within myself that I needed to take a good look at. It takes such great courage to heal those wounds that have ripped wide open again after many hard years of healing work.

We heal and move through layers until the next door of healing presents itself. Instead of running away, we must follow our curiosity and walk toward the light coming through the crack in the slightly opened door. It is inviting us to take another step of courage into the wild terrain of our hearts and sometimes through heartbreaking realities of grief as we climb through the arduous terrain.

I was fully aware that my marriage needed some serious repair. With each step comes hope, faith and a stronger core of the very truth that defines us as humans. I have been constantly reminded throughout my spiritual journey that this is the ultimate path of forgiveness. Forgiving ourselves is the greatest act of self-love. That is what I found here at Spirit Mountain. I don't know what the future holds, or whether my marriage will withstand the great storms as it has in the past, but either way a new story begins, a new chapter is written, and I choose to write it with more love, peace and serenity within my being.

## Bear Medicine

I remember having a terrifying dream of a bear some time ago. I was being devoured by the spirit of a grizzly. Piece by piece I was being dismantled. It left me horror-stricken and confused. After sharing my dream with a medicine man I learned that it was actually not at all frightening. Instead it was empowering and a clear sign of rebirth and renewal. From that moment, I welcomed the bear into my life through journeys and by honoring the bear spirit.

As I have mentioned throughout this book, our spirit allies can be wonderful teachers and protectors. If you allow them to guide you and continue to build a stronger relationship with them, you will be amazed at the profound guidance that you will receive. Not only in the spirit world but you will also see it manifest into your physical reality. Some may say it is just your imagination fabricating this, as we have a powerful mind that can create so many things, but when the guidance is validated in your physical world, you know there are greater forces working their magic.

Shamans and Indigenous people from around the world are aware of this and have been practicing animism for thousands of years. To the spirit of the bear and protector of my family, I thank you for being a fierce force and a beautiful guardian to us all. Thank you for the empowering dreams and for the constant protection and guidance, always giving myself and my family direction. May we continue to dance in this divine dream of oneness. And of course, share lots of blueberries. May all of you be blessed with the guidance and spirit of the bear.

## Wolf Spirit

Since I was a child, I have always had a deep love and connection to the wolf spirit. It was the very first spirit animal that I connected with. It came to me in a dream to save me from a dangerous situation in my early twenties when I was almost lured into a cult. I wrote about this experience in my first book *Awakening the Divine Soul*. The spirit of the wolf also came to me while I was on a Greyhound bus ride from Arizona to Rapid City, South Dakota after being invited to a sun dance that forever changed the course of my life.

While passing through Montana and connecting with the big sky, the clouds began to speak to me. The spirit of a wolf appeared through the shape of the clouds, which, in turn, led me to unveiling more about the wolf spirit. After arriving in Rapid City, I found myself in a beautiful store where a Native American man shared a story about the wolf with me and then gave me a sacred and unexpected wolf gift.

Do you ever see shapes in the clouds? Images that look so real they represent something? Trusting in the journey that you are being guided on is crucial. This will give you clear insight that will enable you to see things more clearly beyond what you have ever imagined. You will enter a portal of great mystery, waiting to reveal the unseen parts of your journey and the hidden aspects of yourself.

It gives me the greatest joy when I am teaching retreats or drumming circles and I see the students' faces light up after encountering their spirit animals for the first time. I have witnessed many transformations and miracles from the beautiful bond with one's spirit allies, and have lived this myself. It is why I continue to teach, and it will always be a great honor for me to offer drumming circles. I would not have been the person I am today if I hadn't stumbled upon my first shamanic weekend retreat over thirty years ago. It has now become a natural daily practice in my life.

To the spirit of the wolf and protector of my family, I am you and you are me. You showed me your true spirit when I was a child. You have guided me through hardships and helped me heal my wounds. I don't have the words to express the immense gratitude and love that I feel. Thank you for always being my guardian, my loyal friend. Thank you for welcoming me into the pack. May our spirits forever be intertwined and may we always stay wild.

Do you have a spirit animal that you feel deeply connected to? Take a moment to thank them, and give them your deepest expression of love and gratitude.

## Enter The Mystery

There is a mystical place within each of us, a place of mystery. If we listen to the nudges within, our outer world will be filled with synchronicities and endless signs from the Universe. That is when you enter the mystery, a place where words cannot define, a force so strong it is undeniable, a wind you don't fight against but surrender to, because you trust the guidance.

When the gust turns into a storm, know that even then you are protected and guided. The journey of mystery is not always filled with rainbows and sunshine. You will gain strength to dance through the hailstorms and the thunder. You will learn to see the beauty through it all and taste the secret.

Keep moving forward and allow your curiosity to take you further down the path to places you have never been. Unwrap the gift you have come to see, be and fulfil. Lift the veil into the unknown, the treasure is waiting for you.

## Turtle Medicine

One of my fondest memories is from a family vacation in Kauai with Andy and the kids. We were driving back to our resort after stocking up with groceries when we spotted hundreds of Hawaiian green sea turtles sunning themselves on the sandy beach of a little cove.

We were able to park the car and there were steps leading down to where the turtles were sunbathing. We were all in awe of these magnificent creatures. They were huge and looked so much larger when not swimming in the ocean. We couldn't believe how many there were, they were everywhere! It was magical to watch them as they came out of the water to chill out on the sand. Always stay open to receiving the blessings as you never know when or where they may present themselves.

The spirit of the turtle teaches us that sometimes we need not exert too much effort trying to get to our destination. If you succumb to the will of the ocean it will move you closer with each passing wave. The journey then becomes effortless as the great mother ocean takes you into her womb and assists you to follow your own natural rhythm. With each breath, and every step, allow yourself to be carried by spirit instead of trying to do everything by yourself. What message does the turtle spirit have for you?

## Chapter Eighteen

# Beaver Blessings

I was in the processes of restructuring this book when, one morning, I had a powerful dream about a beaver. It was one of those dreams that was crystal clear and seemed so very real as if it was actually taking place. Upon waking, the image was so vivid I felt like I was still in the scene.

It was so empowering to watch this beautiful beaver building its dam. I was mesmerized with the skill it took to strategically place all the sticks and logs. In the dream, I could see muddy water flowing next to a riverbank. The beaver was building a home to provide protection for his family. It was a blessing to witness him being so focused and dedicated on his creation. This was the first time I had connected with the beaver as a spirit animal. The timing was perfect; he was so adorable, I just wanted to hug and play with him.

Beaver medicine is known for bringing wisdom and creativity, being persistent and productive. The beaver is a master builder. In what area of your life can you call upon the spirit of the beaver to assist you? Connect with the beaver's energy and ask for its blessings. You may be surprised with what it has to say.

## Re-create Something New

I will wait for you at twilight for this exercise. Will you meet me there? Here we step into a new sunset together to re-create something new. Something you have never built. Step into a magical mystery of oneness with me, as we bask together in glorious rays of newness. Here we will paint a new canvas of your life.

Create an image in your mind of everything that could ever bring you bliss. The space is here and now, in this very moment.

You are creating something mystical, something uniquely yours, your own secret world. Visualize all the colors of your soul and express yourself in ways that you never have before. Extend your joy into this great mystery.

If you feel called to, grab some crayons or paint, and draw the most divine sunset as a way of expressing what you just experienced. If you are a writer, reach for your journal and write how you are feeling with the word 'sunset' as your prompt. These are powerful ways in which you can express and extend your desires. Either one can be a potent method to attract and manifest incredible things in your life.

## Renew Your Spirit

It was 5:55am. Way too early for me to be awake being a night owl. I had only just fallen asleep a few hours ago, but something nudged me to look out of the window and watch the sun rising. It was soul-stirring and serene. Golden rays appeared to be rising out of the earth. The sun began kissing the sky, spreading its radiant cheer to bless the day.

I felt the call to go into a drum journey. I could feel in my solar plexus that one of my spirit allies had a message for me. As the light of dawn started seeping into my room through my curtains, I prepared myself by burning some sage, sweet grass and cedar. I also had some dried lavender with wildflowers. I expressed gratitude to all my spirit guardians along with the earth, sky, ocean and the four directions of the wind. I thanked the Snuneymuxw First Nations and the spirits of the land that I was so privileged to live on, and all my ancestors, and gave thanks for my family and for my life.

I began to shake my sacred black wolf rattle. This is deeply sentimental to me. It was made for me by an incredibly talented and well respected First Nations elder. I then picked up my cougar drum, the hypnotic beat assisting me to drift into a natural altered state.

I found myself looking at my bare feet in the red earth, once more. I could feel the warmth radiating up through the soil. It was a perfect temperature and so soothing. To my left, I saw Lia. She reached out her hand to join mine. In her other hand she was holding a bouquet of yellow and white flowers in a stunning array, a symbol of our friendship. The scent was strong and sweet.

"Remember to breathe in the sweet fragrance of life," she said.

I drew a breath and made a mental note to remember this when going through life's challenges. "Where are we going, Lia?" I asked.

"We are going to the cave," she answered.

I was always excited to see Kauala, but also nervous. I could feel the heat from the sun warming up the day as we walked toward the cave. When we entered, Kauala was sitting in a meditative position, and wearing a white cotton dress. It looked comfortable and light.

"You are free, child," she said joyously. "This is the moment of transition for you. No more wandering of time, travel and purpose. Everything is intertwined into the deeper depths of being. Understand you are getting closer to knowing your own spiritual boundaries. Time, travel and transcendence are all interwoven into the dance through the never-ending cycle of birth and death. This is good, a good transition, but it's very important to recognize the stopping points between time and space, sometimes altering your perception of reality."

She paused for a moment, glancing over to Lia. I was feeling confused as to what was yet to come as it sounded heavy. I was already into a deep dive on this spiritual journey that was like a never-ending roller coaster ride. Sometimes I was able to jump off and, at other times, I happily hopped back on. After thirty years on this mystical journey, I was still surprised and ready for unexpected adventures.

"You will travel to a faraway land and new teachers will begin guiding you," said Lia. "We will still be here to nurture you, we will never leave your side, but you are entering another phase of your existence. The journey will be arduous and your true strength will be tested."

My heart sunk. For a moment I felt like I was being abandoned. They have been such a big part of my spiritual path that I didn't want to begin any new adventures without them. They were part of my beautiful spirit family.

Tears fell from my eyes. I put my hands over my face and tried to stop myself from sobbing. I looked down at the flowers that Lia had placed on the cave floor to ease my grief and as a symbol of our friendship to grasp onto for some hope, even if only for a few, short minutes.

"I don't like goodbyes," I blubbered, my lips rubbing against my teeth and my face soaked by the tears flowing endlessly from my weary eyes.

"We never leave you, there is no sense of time in our world," explained Kauala.

I looked at her with the vulnerable and trusting eyes of a child. I believed her. I took in a deep breath of courage for what was to come.

"Remember your pen, it will help you to find your way whenever you are feeling lost or confused," she continued.

I could visualize the pen in my mind, the purple, magenta and gold looked even more vibrant than I remembered, and the moonstones were shining so bright as if reflecting actual moonlight. Although I felt a little distraught, I was reassured by her wise words and trusted that she would not completely abandon me.

Lia looked at me with a gentle and kind smile. She always had a way of making me feel better with her calming presence.

"Thank you, Kauala," I said, my tears now starting to subside.

I watched her nod her head up and down and she managed

a half smile while scrunching her tiny nose.

As we left the cave, Lia was still carrying the flowers. Clouds began passing in front of the hot sun, as we noticed the beautiful, Indigenous Australian man with the didgeridoo was here waiting to greet us. He was shirtless, wearing cream-colored shorts and around his neck was an animal bone necklace in the shape of an arrow. I was intrigued by it but didn't want to be rude by staring as it was obviously his personal, spiritual talisman.

He told us about some wildfires currently burning in Australia and how this was expanding the heart chakra of the world. He also spoke of bringing the land back to the original people, not only in Australia, but all over the world.

"Our land and people have been abused and neglected," he said. "The earth has to be brought back into balance just like the purity of those flowers. White represents innocence and yellow is for the sunshine radiating and expanding across the world. The whole planet is going through a rebirth and renewal."

I was so happy to hear that we would all be going through this as a whole, but was also aware the journey of rebirth and renewal was not normally an easy one. Like with everything, there is a natural process that one needs to go through.

"The world is healing, and we are all healing too," he continued, while pointing at the ground.

There was a snake moving slowly in a southwesterly direction. It was pure magic! A mystical serpent with all the colors of the rainbow moving through it.

"The Rainbow dancers are coming out to dance again and show our mother earth how much she is loved. It is also a dance of forgiveness to bring the rain to renew and cleanse the earth. It is said to be the giver of life due to its connection to water. The world is cleansing and healing, and there will be many more changes in the earth. We will be illuminated just as the earth will be," Lia explained, while pointing at the sun.

She handed me the flowers, I held them close to my chest. Flowers have always made me happy, ever since I was a child. I could always understand their secret language. Our friend began to bless us with his digeridoo, starting from our feet, then moving it upwards across the rest of our form. My whole body could feel the magic healing powers vibrating through my being.

I glanced up at the sky. It was purple and magenta with golden streaks across it. The same colors of the pen I was gifted by the old sorceress, my friend, my forever guide. I thanked Lia with a huge hug. She held me so tightly and looked into my eyes while reaching out for my right hand. Her grip was firm.

"You will have so many more adventures, do not be afraid of your own power, child," she reassured.

The beat of the drum was calling me back. I reached for my journal and pen.

## Aurora Dance

Streamers dancing in the midnight sky. Magnetic northern lights swirling in their natural rhythm. Liberation breaking through the clouds in an emerald dance. Our eyes watch with wonder like an innocent child, curious about life's mystery. They widen with delight as the graceful green expands through the atmosphere with divine elegance.

The sound of wolves howling from distant mountains awakens the mystery deep within me. It has been here since forever. The night sky reflects all that we are as mystical and radiant beings. You are a blessing, a true gift from nature. Dance with me across the night sky through the greatest expression of your soul. The search is over, the truth staring right in front of you. Celebrate your creation and expand into your brilliance. Dance the Aurora dance.

## Celebration Ceremony

"Tundra, is that you?" I called out.

I could feel her energy close to me. The beat of the drum was pounding through my heart as I travelled so quickly on a sled through a tunnel filled with glossy, icy snow. I gripped tightly onto the sides, trying desperately not to fall off as I made my way rapidly through this portal. I arrived at the other end unscathed into a wintry scene with thick snowflakes decorating the already breathtaking landscape. I stuck my tongue out to catch one, feeling like a little girl once again.

Amazed by the scene, I walked out among the giant snowflakes, looking for my friend.

"Tundra, it's me, where are you?" I called again.

I captured an image of her, peeking out from behind a snowbank, high up on the hillside. My eyes squinted to get a clearer view as the snow continued to fall heavily. The moon greeted me in her fullness as I made my way up the hill toward my friend, crunching through the snow and leaving behind a trail of deep footprints. The crisp air was still, as the flurry continued to grace the earth. My Arctic fox now came to join me as I found myself knee high into the snow.

I could see Tundra's ears pricking up as I approached her. My fox was jumping with excitement and encouraging me to keep going. I made it to the top to be rewarded by the most incredible sight. There were three small cubs with Tundra! She looked incredibly proud, standing so tall, protecting them. She was now a mother. I could see the love and gratification radiating through her eyes as she showed off her wonderful achievement to me.

"You made it, and you listened to my advice," she said.

I ran to her with open arms and wrapped them around her neck. I rubbed my face against her soft fur nestling my head against her powerful body. It felt so real, our connection was genuine, a special bond that could never be broken. Her cubs began to jump all over me, playing so joyfully. I was now in complete bliss, frolicking with her three adorable cubs with endless cuddles from these cute bundles of fur. My fox even joined in on this love fest.

The snow had subsided to a light dusting and the moon was bright, lighting up the whole hilltop. The stars blinked in the sky, it was a perfect and joyful reunion.

"Be proud of the path you have chosen," Tundra told me in a soft tone. "Remember to have pride in everything you do, own your story and embrace your uniqueness. Every word that you speak matters, so choose wisely and remember that you are never alone. Even if you find yourself in dark places, the moon will always be there to light up the pathway like it is now. You will go on many adventures through the galaxy of imagination and wonder. Journey with the stars as they carry many surprises and will bring you much joy."

"I love you, Tundra, thank you for being with me on this incredible journey of life," I said through tears of joy while giving her the biggest bear hug.

We sat and cuddled together as we watched the stars twinkling above us and occasionally plummeting to earth, leaving a trail of sparkling light in their wake. My Arctic fox and the three bear cubs were snuggled beside us. It was like having the warmest, softest blanket around me, filled with so much affection. This was a very special kind of celebration ceremony, as we rejoiced in the birth of her cubs, the new life that she had brought into creation. I was truly grateful and felt so deeply loved.

What will you celebrate today? Look at how far you have come on your own journey. Honor and celebrate in whatever way you chose in a sacred ceremony. You can gather your favorite flowers, crystals, rocks or any other objects to use in a meditation, prayer or ritual. You may want to journey to your spirit allies and invite them to celebrate with you. They might even have special instructions for you. It is important to honor and acknowledge every part of your journey.

## Back in the Igloo

The view below us was heavenly, an open landscape of snow-capped mountains, frozen lakes and icebergs. I could see an igloo lit up, not too far in the distance. I knew it was my dear guides who were waiting for me. The moon was leaving a silvery trail, like snail tracks, leading straight to the igloo.

I said goodbye to Tundra and her precious cubs, kissing them all on the cheeks. I intuitively knew I would see them again. My fox and I walked down the hillside toward the igloo. We could see stunning streamers of green, red and yellow in the sky. It was the northern lights blessing us with an alluring display. I breathed the essence of the aurora borealis into my being and could feel the gratitude radiating all through my cells.

I entered the igloo and was met by my spirit parents. It was cozy and warm inside as a small fire was burning in the center. My Arctic fox was sitting beside me to my left. She is small and gentle but has hidden power. She reminds me of independence and also to continue inviting playfulness into everything I do, not taking things too seriously. My spirit teachers held both my hands so tightly. They looked me in the eyes reminding me of their continuous love, guidance and support.

"This fire will keep burning for you as we continue to assist you on many new adventures. More books will be written," said my spirit mother.

I looked at my spirit father, our eyes locked with a deep love and acceptance. My heart was full. He always has a way of taking me into a deep state of tranquility.

I was now ready to move into the next phase of my journey and start writing the next book. As always, I will wait for the nudge, the signs and synchronicities that will follow. Trusting in my spirit allies is key. They have led me on the most incredible journeys of my life. The adventures in the spirit world have always been validated for me in my physical world. I could not be more grateful.

They both looked at me, sincerely through my heart and soul.

"You are learning how to nurture yourself more and are now ready to write your next books," she continued.

I looked at her and nodded my head in agreement, as I was now ready to move forward without being so hard on myself. I also understood how crucial it was to have a date with myself, to take more time to replenish and revitalize my energy.

"You are still finding your equilibrium. Many new teachers will enter your life, some will come, and some will go," she went on, while looking at me through smiling eyes.

"I can't thank you both enough for all you have done for me; you have completely transformed my life from the very start," I told them, with tears of gratitude trickling down my face. "I love you both dearly, thank you again."

My fox left the igloo and I soon followed her. The moon was still beaming so beautifully above us, the stars blinking in acknowledgement. I took in a deep breath soaking up every inch of the glorious scene.

I could feel my body becoming lighter as I continued to breathe in the essence of the night sky. The aurora was now emerald green merging with golden yellow. With every breath, my cells and entire body captured the luminescence. I felt a completion of the old path as the colors spiraled through my body in a transformation of renewal and rebirth. This journey was complete. I drew in another breath of courage, filled my lungs with fresh energy, a new vitality for the next adventure I would soon be entering.

I could hear a whisper in the wind with these words, "We need to keep love alive in order to thrive. Our planet needs love to live and so do we."

I thought about all the times I could have let in more love. We can all allow more love to enter our lives. I am starting to recreate myself as if a new part of me is being born, a part of me that I have never known.

There is a deep part of you that you never knew existed. Do you hear the call to re-create? Open your heart and invite love to enter. Breathe in gratitude for all that you are. Now is your time to dig even deeper to discover who you truly are. Are you ready for your new journey of rebirth and renewal?

Enter your imagination, invite your creative visualization to expand into new depths of being that are aligned with your truest heart's desires. Take a step of courage into your new life. The starting point is now.

## Meeting with a Mystic

The clock read 3:33am. The image of an old, thin Indian man with white hair started to fade. I woke up in a sweat, my nightgown drenched, and my heart pounding. I reached for my water as I was feeling nauseous. I took a sip and my heartbeat started to slow. I felt a tug at my solar plexus as I started to remember part of the dream. I could still hear his voice echoing through me.

"Time to change your destiny," he whispered.

He was firmly holding my right hand up to his face. His eyes focused closely at my lifeline.

"Was I going to die?" I thought to myself. "Was this a warning of some kind? Maybe it was just a crazy dream, or maybe this man was real, a mystic who wanted to help and guide me."

Since I was a little girl, I often wondered how much time I would have on this earth. How long do any of us have left in this lifetime?

I then recalled these words he had spoken to me, "I am real, come find me."

If this man truly did exist and was still alive, then I knew I had to find him. One of the clues in the dream was that I knew for sure he lived in India. I would plan a trip later that same year and the search would begin...

# Afterword ~ Continue the Journey

As I pick up my drum and the book comes to a close, each beat I play is for you and your new journey. Can you feel the pulse? With every beat I am sending you gratitude, love and serenity. My greatest wish is that you live your truest and deepest heart's desires.

Align your heartbeat with that of mother earth. Imagine you are standing with your favorite tree. Feel the strength and support coming from the earth as your feet are firmly planted and your back is resting against the trunk. Deeply breathe into the source of your natural rhythm. It is springtime within the meadow of your soul, and wildflowers are blossoming so abundantly. Hummingbirds are drinking the sweet nectar while butterflies gracefully dance from flower to flower. Be still in your courage and feel the power within you.

I honor and thank you for being on this adventure with me. May you have so many beautiful and bountiful blessings along the way. If at any time you find yourself diverting or moving out of your natural rhythm, come back to yourself and realign into your own inherent flow. Focus on your heart and center yourself in the breath of life.

Your authentic self will never steer you the wrong way. Be true to who you are. Only then will you find your rightful path. Look beyond the horizon, as here lays the most magnificent reflection of you. Call out to all of your spirit animals and invite them to sing, dance, write, draw, play and celebrate your new journey with you. Congratulations on coming so far on your unique, mystical journey of rebirth and renewal. I celebrate you now and always.

Love, Rosanna xo

# Acknowledgements

I would first like to thank the Creator, my mother Carmela and my father Giuseppe for bringing me into creation.

Thank you, Ma, for being my Shero and for teaching me the true meaning of strength, resilience and independence. You are a true Warrior Goddess Survivor, and I love you so much.

Thank you, Papa, for guiding my spirit for so many years. I know you continue to sail freely into the sunset. Free at last, I love you.

To my husband Andy, we survived another first draft edit, fifteen years since the last one, over thirty years together, raising our three incredible children and still married after twenty-two years. We have moved through rough storms, well more like hurricanes at times, seen the worst and the best of one another. I know there are many rainbows waiting on the horizon for us. We keep growing and evolving together. Being soul mates doesn't always mean bliss, even though we sure know how to laugh hysterically together, but I'm always a believer, and an optimist and know we both deserve more of that. This book is all about rebirth and renewal, and that includes our marriage. Here's to more adventures, laughter and joy. Thank you for having my back. I couldn't have finished this book without you. I love you with all of my heart.

To my beloved three children Keanu, Aragorn and Amethyst. Thank you for the beauty, the blessings, lessons and the unconditional love that you bring to me. It is such an honor to be your mother. Watching you grow into such passionate, kind, loving and incredibly creative and unique individuals is such a joy. Whatever path you choose in life, be happy and keep nurturing your passion. Fulfilment comes from within. You are the loves of my life. I can't wait to go on many more adventures together and create even more memories. I love you all to eternity. Remember to always keep your dreams alive.

To my siblings Dominic, Virg, Sam and Mary. Thank you for your uniqueness, creativity and great taste in music. I feel so blessed to have been raised with such incredible diverse music. We should have formed a band together! For our laughter, tears and crazy, fun times, the deep journeys and conversations, the love and the humor, I love you. Oh, and the stories we could tell our children...

To all of my spirit allies, power animals, sages, mystics, angels and wise ones. I am deeply humbled by the great mystery. I thank you with all of my heart and soul for your endless guidance and protection on this mystical life journey.

To my publisher John Hunt, for believing in me back in 2007. You gave me so much encouragement by telling me that you liked my style. For a complete beginner and dyslexic, that meant the world to me. That was the beginning of my writing journey. Your words meant more to me than you will ever know. I am forever grateful.

To my dear friend Victoria Sheridan, thank you for your wonderful friendship, love and many blessings over the twenty-five years we have known each other. Your support and encouragement over the years has been endless. I am truly grateful and look forward to future projects together.

To my dear friend Roz Selim, what a journey it has been! I am forever grateful for our friendship for over twenty-eight years and for the continued love, support and spiritual guidance. We will be forever laughing with the cosmos.

To my dear friend Bruce, thank you for your friendship and constant support over the past twenty-eight years. You know you are part of the pack.

To my dear friend Clark Salsa Mantei, my music and concert buddy. I can't thank you enough for your creative genius, your friendship and the endless heart to heart conversations. Mr. Plant played the *Rain Song* and tears fell from my eyes! I will never ever forget that fate-filled day when we met Robert Plant. My heart-to-heart conversation with him will live with me forever! Having lunch across the table from him and Paul Rodgers was really cool too!

To my dear friend Liz, for over thirty-eight years of friendship and for all the times you had my back... I will be forever grateful. No matter how many years go by, you remain in my heart. The love between Soul Friends never fades.

For my old friend Anthony, all those corrections you made with my spelling over the years in early letters... hopefully I can spell much better now (insert a big smile). Thank you for the soul conversations over the years.

To my beautiful high school friend Michelle, for the years of laughter, tears, heart and soul and so much fun! The Twilight Zone days were epic. We had such incredible memories... the tales we could tell. You are amazing and fierce... you so got this! I love you dearly.

To my very first best friend Stacey, I still can't believe I have known you since I was five years old. Thank you for the fun early years and for helping me to express my imagination. Playing teacher and playing with pine needles and berries pretending we were doctors was so much fun along with all the other crazy things we did. And for your beautiful mother Lynda who was like a second mom to me, thank you for the love and kindness.

There are too many more friends to thank here... I haven't forgotten you. Please forgive me and know I love and appreciate you and our friendship. Thank you for being in my life.

To all of my dear students and clients, thank you for putting your trust in me. You are such wonderful teachers. It is my deep honor and joy to continue to be of the best service to you. Keep sharing your love and beauty with the world.

To my soul sisters on the Magical Mystery Tour of Sedona and the Southwest. I will never forget our sacred time together. It truly was magical. Each and every one of you will be in my heart forever. For our beautiful soul sister Leslie, you are amongst the stars, shining so brightly as you did here on earth, but I will remember your gorgeous smile, your deep love and magical bond with your sister Linda and pure heart playing the hummingbird drum to eternity. I love you.

To all my loved ones in spirit, thank you for your constant guidance. I continue to hear you loud and clear. I miss you terribly and love you so very dearly.

To Jesse Kalu for taking me safely to all the sacred caves. Your generosity and gorgeous flute sounds will forever stay in my heart. Thank you for helping to open the portal of this book for me over ten years ago.

To Jolynn, my dear soul sister. Thank you for all the sacred adventures we shared together in Sedona, through Arizona and in Banff and Lake Louise. I will never forget the full moon ceremony and the motorcycle ride in Monument Valley.

To Layla, my soul sister, thank you for the many adventures we have shared over the years. The Magical Mystery Tours and our sacred time at Spirit Ridge Resort. We are always in the right place at the right time.

Thank you to Elaine for all those wonderful EFT tapping sessions together. So much magic happened in your healing room and the unexpected wisdom of Wayne Dyer. I am truly grateful.

Thank you to my acupuncturist Clayton Willoughby for helping to balance my health with all the sessions. Some wonderful meditation journeys happened in your clinic.

Thank you to my chiropractor Dr. Glen Reed for helping me to get my health back on track. I was in so much pain when I first came to see you all those years ago.

Thank you to my beloved teacher Dr. Clarissa Pinkola Estés, I am so very grateful for everything you have given to me. I feel so blessed to have studied the Mysterium Psychology with you. You completely transformed my life. I love you with all my heart and soul. Siempre xo.

Thank you to the late and great Bob Proctor. You truly were an extraordinary gentleman. I will be forever grateful to you for helping me to shift my paradigms, giving me a clearer mindset and seeing that all things are possible. It really meant the world to me when you endorsed my first book.

Thank you to Dr. Gabor Maté for helping me to become more grounded and present with my trauma through Compassionate Inquiry.

Thank you to Ann Randolph for helping me to Unmute Myself. I truly appreciate your love, support, humor, raw and real presence. You Rock!

Thank you to Julia Cameron. *The Artist's Way* has changed my life.

Thank you to Natalie Goldberg for helping me to find my true voice through writing.

Thank you to David Whyte for further opening the portals to my inner poet.

I want to thank and acknowledge the Snuneymuxw First Nation people for allowing us the privilege to live, work and play on your sacred territory. I give my deep thanks to all the First Peoples throughout Vancouver Island and Canada, the peoples of the Arctic, the Inuit, the Native American people, and the Indigenous people from Australia and all over the world for the privilege of walking on your sacred lands. My deepest gratitude to our dear Mother Earth, may we all learn to take better care of you.

# About the Author

Rosanna is a wife, mother of three children and Award-Winning Finalist of the 2010 International Book Awards, 2010 National Indie Excellence Awards, 2009 National Best Books Awards and the best-selling author of *Awakening the Divine Soul: Finding Your Life Purpose*. She is an ordained minister with a Bachelor's degree in metaphysical science and is pursuing a PhD in Philosophy, specializing in mystical research. She is also the founder of Motivational Mentoring for the Soul.

Having overcome her own personal traumas and obstacles, she has dedicated her life to serving clients and students from around the world with her workshops, programs and retreats. She has been studying Shamanic arts, Spirituality, Psychism and Mysticism for over thirty years. Rosanna offers empowerment workshops, shamanic drumming circles, online programs, mentoring programs, intuitive soul readings and has healing practices on Vancouver Island, the UK and in Europe. Her spiritual journey has taken her through many parts of the world where she learned and sat with Shamans, Medicine men and women, and Mystics. Rosanna is a visionary who uses her gifts of deep insight to enhance the lives of others.

# Resources

www.visitarizona.com
www.visitsedona.com
www.banfflakelouise.com
www.indigenousbc.com
www.anchorinn.ca
https://nkmipdesert.com

*Women Who Run With the Wolves: Myths and Stories of the Wild Woman Archetype*
Dr. Clarissa Pinkola Estés
www.clarissapinkolaestes.com

*The Artist's Way: A Spiritual Path to Higher Creativity*
Julia Cameron
www.juliacameronlive.com

*Writing Down the Bones*
Natalie Goldberg
https://nataliegoldberg.com

*Pilgrim*
David Whyte
www.davidwhyte.com

*Your Story Matters: Unmute Yourself*
Ann Randolph
www.annrandolph.com

*The Myth of Normal with Daniel Maté: Trauma, Illness & Healing in a Toxic Culture*
Dr. Gabor Maté

www.drgabormate.com

*It Didn't Start with You: How Inherited Family Trauma Shapes Who We Are and How to End the Cycle*
Mark Wolynn
www.markwolynn.com

*You Were Born Rich*
*Change Your Paradigm: Change Your Life*
Bob Proctor
www.proctorgallagherinstitute.com

*Awakening the Divine Soul: Finding Your Life Purpose*
*Awakening Your Divine Soul: 11 Steps to Finding Your Life Purpose 6 CD Set*
Rosanna Ienco
www.themysticoracle.com

*Eat-Clean Cookbook*
*Eat-Clean Diet Series*
Tosca Reno
www.toscareno.com

*Soul Coaching: The Ultimate Inner and Outer Clutter Clearing Program*
*Kindling the Native Spirit: Sacred Practices for Everyday Life*
*Past Lives: Present Miracles*
Denise Linn
www.deniselinnseminars.com

*Messages from Spirit: The Extraordinary Power of Oracles, Omens, and Signs*
Colette Baron-Reid
www.colettebaronreid.com

212

*Rejuvenate Your Life*
Victoria Sheridan
Rejuvenation and Lifestyle Coach
www.victoriasheridancoach.com

*Savy Wisdom: It Has the Power to Change Your Life*
*Savy Wisdom 2: The Sequel*
Peggy McColl
https://go.peggymccoll.com

The Scandinavian Center for Shamanic Studies
www.shamanism.dk

*The Way of the Shaman*
Michael Harner
The Foundation for Shamanic Studies
www.shamanism.org

*Soul Retrieval: Mending the Fragmented Self*
*Shamanic Journeying: A Beginner's Guide*
*Medicine for the Earth: How to Transform Personal and Environmental*
*    Toxins*
Sandra Ingerman
www.sandraingerman.com

*Conscious Dreaming: A Spiritual Path for Everyday Life*
Robert Moss
www.mossdreams.com

*Healing Journeys with the Black Madonna: Chants, Music, and*
*    Sacred Practices of the Great Goddess*
Alessandra Belloni
www.alessandrabelloni.com

In memory of our dear Goddess sister Cher Lyn
www.mysticartmedicine.com
www.chocolatree.com

Debut album: *Celestial Desire*
Keanu Ienco
www.keanuienco.com

Jesse Kalu
www.jessekalu.hearnow.com

# O-BOOKS

# SPIRITUALITY

O is a symbol of the world, of oneness and unity; this eye represents knowledge and insight. We publish titles on general spirituality and living a spiritual life. We aim to inform and help you on your own journey in this life.
If you have enjoyed this book, why not tell other readers by posting a review on your preferred book site?

## Recent bestsellers from O-Books are:

### Heart of Tantric Sex
Diana Richardson
Revealing Eastern secrets of deep love and intimacy to Western couples.
Paperback: 978-1-90381-637-0 ebook: 978-1-84694-637-0

### Crystal Prescriptions
The A-Z guide to over 1,200 symptoms and their healing crystals
Judy Hall
The first in the popular series of eight books, this handy little guide is packed as tight as a pill-bottle with crystal remedies for ailments.
Paperback: 978-1-90504-740-6 ebook: 978-1-84694-629-5

## Take Me To Truth
Undoing the Ego
Nouk Sanchez, Tomas Vieira
The best-selling step-by-step book on shedding the Ego, using the
teachings of *A Course In Miracles*.
Paperback: 978-1-84694-050-7 ebook: 978-1-84694-654-7


## The 7 Myths about Love...Actually!
The Journey from your HEAD to the HEART of your SOUL
Mike George
Smashes all the myths about LOVE.
Paperback: 978-1-84694-288-4 ebook: 978-1-84694-682-0


## The Holy Spirit's Interpretation of the New Testament
A Course in Understanding and Acceptance
Regina Dawn Akers
Following on from the strength of *A Course In Miracles*, NTI
teaches us how to experience the love and oneness of God.
Paperback: 978-1-84694-085-9 ebook: 978-1-78099-083-5


## The Message of A Course In Miracles
A translation of the Text in plain language
Elizabeth A. Cronkhite
A translation of *A Course In Miracles* into plain, everyday
language for anyone seeking inner peace. The companion
volume, *Practicing A Course In Miracles*, offers practical lessons
and mentoring.
Paperback: 978-1-84694-319-5 ebook: 978-1-84694-642-4

## Your Simple Path
Find Happiness in every step
Ian Tucker
A guide to helping us reconnect with what is really important in
our lives.
Paperback: 978-1-78279-349-6 ebook: 978-1-78279-348-9

## 365 Days of Wisdom
Daily Messages To Inspire You Through The Year
Dadi Janki
Daily messages which cool the mind, warm the heart and guide
you along your journey.
Paperback: 978-1-84694-863-3 ebook: 978-1-84694-864-0

## Body of Wisdom
Women's Spiritual Power and How it Serves
Hilary Hart
Bringing together the dreams and experiences of women across
the world with today's most visionary spiritual teachers.
Paperback: 978-1-78099-696-7 ebook: 978-1-78099-695-0

## Dying to Be Free
From Enforced Secrecy to Near Death to True Transformation
Hannah Robinson
After an unexpected accident and near-death experience, Hannah
Robinson found herself radically transforming her life, while a
remarkable new insight altered her relationship with her father, a
practising Catholic priest.
Paperback: 978-1-78535-254-6 ebook: 978-1-78535-255-3

## The Ecology of the Soul
A Manual of Peace, Power and Personal Growth for Real People
in the Real World
Aidan Walker
Balance your own inner Ecology of the Soul to regain your
natural state of peace, power and wellbeing.
Paperback: 978-1-78279-850-7 ebook: 978-1-78279-849-1

## Not I, Not other than I
The Life and Teachings of Russel Williams
Steve Taylor, Russel Williams
The miraculous life and inspiring teachings of one of the World's
greatest living Sages.
Paperback: 978-1-78279-729-6 ebook: 978-1-78279-728-9

## On the Other Side of Love
A woman's unconventional journey towards wisdom
Muriel Maufroy
When life has lost all meaning, what do you do?
Paperback: 978-1-78535-281-2 ebook: 978-1-78535-282-9

## Practicing A Course In Miracles
A translation of the Workbook in plain language, with
mentor's notes
Elizabeth A. Cronkhite
The practical second and third volumes of The Plain-Language
*A Course In Miracles.*
Paperback: 978-1-84694-403-1 ebook: 978-1-78099-072-9

## Quantum Bliss
The Quantum Mechanics of Happiness, Abundance, and Health
George S. Mentz
*Quantum Bliss* is the breakthrough summary of success and spirituality secrets that customers have been waiting for.
Paperback: 978-1-78535-203-4 ebook: 978-1-78535-204-1

## The Upside Down Mountain
Mags MacKean
A must-read for anyone weary of chasing success and happiness – one woman's inspirational journey swapping the uphill slog for the downhill slope.
Paperback: 978-1-78535-171-6 ebook: 978-1-78535-172-3

## Your Personal Tuning Fork
The Endocrine System
Deborah Bates
Discover your body's health secret, the endocrine system, and 'twang' your way to sustainable health!
Paperback: 978-1-84694-503-8 ebook: 978-1-78099-697-4

Readers of ebooks can buy or view any of these bestsellers by clicking on the live link in the title. Most titles are published in paperback and as an ebook. Paperbacks are available in traditional bookshops. Both print and ebook formats are available online.
Find more titles and sign up to our readers' newsletter at
http://www.johnhuntpublishing.com/mind-body-spirit
Follow us on Facebook at https://www.facebook.com/OBooks/
and Twitter at https://twitter.com/obooks